THE BEDFORD SERIES IN HISTORY AND CULTURE

Welfare Reform
in the Early Republic

A Brief History with Documents

W9-BGK-000

Related Titles in
THE BEDFORD SERIES IN HISTORY AND CULTURE
Advisory Editors: Natalie Zemon Davis, Princeton University
Ernest R. May, Harvard University
Lynn Hunt, University of California, Los Angeles
David W. Blight, Yale University

THE BEDFORD SERIES IN HISTORY AND CULTURE

Welfare Reform in the Early Republic

A Brief History with Documents

Seth Rockman

Occidental College

BEDFORD/ST. MARTIN'S   Boston ◆ New York

To my students, colleagues, and friends at Occidental College

For Bedford/St. Martin's

Publisher for History: Patricia A. Rossi
Director of Development for History: Jane Knetzger
Associate Developmental Editor: Amy McConathy Langlais
Editorial Assistant: Rachel Siegel
Editorial Assistant, Publishing Services: Maria Teresa Burwell
Senior Production Supervisor: Dennis J. Conroy
Production Associate: Christie Gross
Marketing Manager: Jenna Bookin Barry
Project Management: Books By Design, Inc.
Text Design: Claire Seng-Niemoeller
Indexer: Books By Design, Inc.
Cover Design: Billy Boardman
Cover Photo: The Drunkard's Progress, or, The Direct Road to Poverty, Wretchedness, & Ruin, 1826. Library of Congress, Rare Books and Special Collections Division, Printed Ephemera Collection, Portfolio 6, Folder 23.
Composition: Stratford Publishing Services, Inc.
Printing and Binding: Haddon Craftsmen, an RR Donnelley & Sons Company

President: Joan E. Feinberg
Director of Marketing: Karen R. Melton
Director of Editing, Design, and Production: Marcia Cohen
Manager, Publishing Services: Emily Berleth

Library of Congress Control Number: 2002103902

Manufactured in the United States of America.

7 6 5 4 3 2 1 0
f e d

For information, write: Bedford/St. Martin's, 75 Arlington Street, Boston, MA 02116 (617-399-4000)

ISBN-10: 0-312-39821-2
ISBN-13: 978-0-312-39821-7

Foreword

The Bedford Series in History and Culture is designed so that readers can study the past as historians do.

The historian's first task is finding the evidence. Documents, letters, memoirs, interviews, pictures, movies, novels, or poems can provide facts and clues. Then the historian questions and compares the sources. There is more to do than in a courtroom, for hearsay evidence is welcome, and the historian is usually looking for answers beyond act and motive. Different views of an event may be as important as a single verdict. How a story is told may yield as much information as what it says.

Along the way the historian seeks help from other historians and perhaps from specialists in other disciplines. Finally, it is time to write, to decide on an interpretation and how to arrange the evidence for readers.

Each book in this series contains an important historical document or group of documents, each document a witness from the past and open to interpretation in different ways. The documents are combined with some element of historical narrative—an introduction or a biographical essay, for example—that provides students with an analysis of the primary source material and important background information about the world in which it was produced.

Each book in the series focuses on a specific topic within a specific historical period. Each provides a basis for lively thought and discussion about several aspects of the topic and the historian's role. Each is short enough (and inexpensive enough) to be a reasonable one-week assignment in a college course. Whether as classroom or personal reading, each book in the series provides firsthand experience of the challenge—and fun—of discovering, recreating, and interpreting the past.

Natalie Zemon Davis
Ernest R. May
Lynn Hunt
David W. Blight

Preface

Almost as soon as Lyndon Johnson declared war on poverty in 1964, welfare reform became a hot-button issue in American politics. Virtually every presidential campaign of the last four decades has addressed social spending for the poor. Promises to "end welfare as we know it" and slogans like "compassionate conservatism" have propelled both Republican and Democratic candidates into the White House. On the state level, Californians approved ballot initiatives to limit public services to illegal immigrants, while Wisconsin made food stamps and monetary aid contingent upon work. In New York City, welfare recipients can be found cleaning parks and subway stations in exchange for benefits. In cities around the country, quality-of-life ordinances have been used to arrest the homeless. As the provisions of the 1996 "Personal Responsibility and Work Opportunity Reconciliation Act"—better known as the Welfare Reform Act—are now taking effect, Americans, rich and poor, are waiting to see what will happen. The topic of welfare reform could not be timelier.

Although the phrase "welfare reform" is modern, the documents in this volume show that the sentiment is not. In the decades between the American Revolution and the 1840s, politicians, clergy, newspaper editors, economists, labor activists, and the poor themselves agreed that reformulating public and private relief programs was essential to the nation's survival. But there was great disagreement as to the causes of poverty. The debate pitted those who saw poverty as a matter of personal moral failing against those who located poverty in the structural weaknesses of the capitalist economy. Proposed "reforms" included institutionalizing the poor in prison-like almshouses, providing them with job training, or leaving them to fend for themselves in a free-market economy.

The rhetoric of the early republic welfare reform debate is alarmingly familiar, but the documents in this volume are not intended to suggest that nothing has changed in 200 years. Rather, by asking why the topic of poor relief generated so much attention at a given moment in history, we can identify the broader political, cultural, economic, and social features of an entire era. In this volume, welfare reform serves as a vehicle for understanding how early republic Americans addressed the issues of their time. The introduction seeks to guide readers through the legacies of the American Revolution, the challenges of an emergent capitalist economy, the religious imperatives of the Second Great Awakening, and the formation of class, gender, and racial identities.

The documents collected in Part Two span the years 1797 to 1838 and come primarily from the Atlantic seaboard cities of Boston, New York, Philadelphia, and Baltimore. Then, like now, rural poverty constituted a serious problem, but garnered less attention as the public eye focused on the habits of the urban poor. The documents include moral reform tracts, almshouse records, and radical plans for property redistribution. Read critically and against the grain, such documents tell us a great deal about the men and women who created them, as well as about working-class and impoverished Americans.

ACKNOWLEDGMENTS

I would like to thank Patricia Rossi and David Blight for their support of this project. Fellow Bedford/St. Martin's authors Victoria Brown, Lynn Dumenil, and Jonathan Earle provided encouragement, as did sales representative Stacy Luce. Amy Langlais patiently guided the manuscript through production. Derek Lynn and Crystal Tomlin assisted with typing. The Gilder Lehrman Institute funded a month's research at The New-York Historical Society. Much of the work on this project was completed at the Library Company of Philadelphia, where Connie King and Jenny Ambrose located compelling pamphlets and illustrations with great enthusiasm and expertise. No research library houses a more friendly or competent staff. Lori Ginzberg, Daniel Dupre, Stephen Mintz, Gary Kornblith, and Jamie Bronstein were very generous critics, as was Shawn Kimmel, whose research time at the Library Company overlapped with mine. Josh Greenberg heroically suggested useful documents on working-class politics. Tara Nummedal was wonderful in every way. Students in my Fall 2000 History 101 course worked through many of these documents, and I learned a great deal from such budding historians as Anthony Truong, Kendall Smith,

Aaron Feldman, Lydia Sargent, and Kyleen Lee. I dedicate this book to Occidental College, where the pursuit of social and economic justice animates campus life and guides how members of its community learn, teach, and work.

Seth Rockman

Contents

23. Mulhearn, *New Answers to the Woman Who...*, Letter 1871.
24. *The Australian Hotel in England* (1964) see file TK43.
25. United public National Library, On B... see above table.

APPENDIXES

Illustrations

Illustrations

Welfare Reform
in the Early Republic

A Brief History with Documents

PART ONE

Introduction: Poverty "in a Land Flowing with Milk and Honey"

What responsibility does society have toward those who are unable to find work, feed their families, or stay warm during a freezing winter? Elected officials, concerned taxpayers, devout clergymen, militant workers, and the poor themselves debated this question as the number of needy Americans grew rapidly in the first decades of the nineteenth century. Few agreed on the causes of poverty or responded with the same sense of moral obligation, religious duty, or fiscal responsibility. The only common understanding was that existing methods of providing relief—whether through government programs or private charity— were failing.

Between the drafting of the Constitution in 1787 and a financial depression starting in 1837, poverty was the most pressing social issue facing the United States. During those fifty years, an older belief in the inevitability of poverty gave way to a new imperative to banish poverty altogether from society. The urgency of eradicating poverty— as well as the optimism that such a thing was possible—had roots in Enlightenment rationalism, Protestant evangelism, and American exceptionalism. Indeed, confidence in human reason and faith in the necessity of erecting God's kingdom on earth combined to convince

1

Americans that their nation—alone among nations—could escape poverty and the attendant curses of social conflict, moral decay, and political corruption.

Poverty was no abstraction for the men, women, and children who struggled against hunger, exposure, and disease in the alleys of cities like Boston, New York, Philadelphia, and Baltimore. Over 90 percent of Americans still lived in rural areas, but as cities multiplied in the early nineteenth century, so too did the number of urban families dependent on wages for their livelihoods. Winter freezes, summer epidemics, and unpredictable stoppages in commerce made it difficult to earn a steady income. No minimum-wage law guaranteed laboring families enough money to cover the growing costs of food, fuel, and rent. Many impoverished households depended on governmental assistance to stay afloat. Public relief supplemented the wages of family members in addition to their participation in underground networks of trade and barter and their reliance upon scavenging, private charity, and begging. Week-to-week survival proved a challenge often lost, as evidenced by the growing population residing in almshouses, or institutions for the poor. Although the level of abject poverty in the United States was not as great as in London or Mexico City, this was no consolation to those searching for their next meal. As Philadelphia publisher Mathew Carey explained, "Such a state of things, in a prosperous country—'a land flowing with milk and honey,'—is a national disgrace."[1]

Poverty was also a very real problem for public officials, political thinkers, and beleaguered taxpayers. Like Mathew Carey, the town leaders of Hartford, Connecticut, considered poverty out of place "in a country furnished like ours, with such an abundance of the fruits of the earth, and such ample means of comfortable livelihood."[2] The growth of poverty was more than just a curious anomaly: It threatened to break local budgets. In Salem, Massachusetts, for example, expenditures on the poor accounted for nearly 50 percent of the town's 1816 budget. (See Figure 1.) Officials worried that generous relief programs encouraged the poor to live on the public's expense. More alarming, paupers openly mocked the values of thrift, sobriety, and self-control. To a vocal group of early republic politicians, clergy, and philanthropists, the health of the new nation hinged on reforming public welfare programs and, ultimately, on reforming the poor themselves.

Approaching the evidence of welfare reform in the early republic as historians, we must recognize that *reform* is a value-laden word. Despite its connotation of improvement, a reform in public policy does

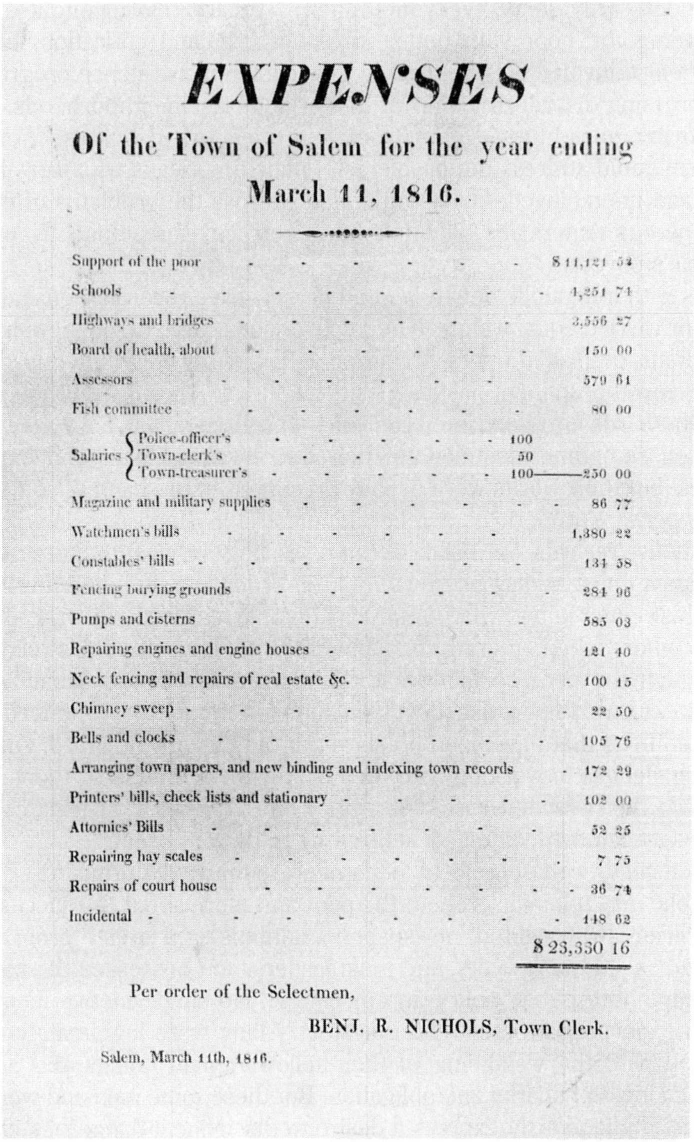

EXPENSES

Of the Town of Salem for the year ending March 11, 1816.

Support of the poor	$11,121 54
Schools	4,251 74
Highways and bridges	3,556 27
Board of health, about	150 00
Assessors	579 61
Fish committee	80 00
Salaries { Police-officer's 100 / Town-clerk's 50 / Town-treasurer's 100	250 00
Magazine and military supplies	86 77
Watchmen's bills	1,380 22
Constables' bills	134 58
Fencing burying grounds	284 96
Pumps and cisterns	585 03
Repairing engines and engine houses	121 40
Neck fencing and repairs of real estate &c.	100 15
Chimney sweep	22 50
Bells and clocks	105 76
Arranging town papers, and new binding and indexing town records	172 29
Printers' bills, check lists and stationary	102 00
Attornies' Bills	52 25
Repairing hay scales	7 75
Repairs of court house	36 74
Incidental	148 62
	$23,330 16

Per order of the Selectmen,

BENJ. R. NICHOLS, Town Clerk.

Salem, March 11th, 1816.

Figure 1. *Urban Budgets.*
Expenses of the town of Salem for the year ending March 11, 1816.
Courtesy, American Antiquarian Society.

3

not necessarily serve everyone equally. Welfare reform might entail providing the poor with better jobs, housing, and education, but it might also involve massive cuts in governmental assistance programs, suppressing disorderly behavior in working-class neighborhoods, and removing unsightly beggars from gentrified urban spaces. Welfare reform could address the problems of poor Americans who were hungry and unemployed, but it could also address the problems of more prosperous Americans who felt burdened and threatened by other people's poverty.

As with any public debate, not all perspectives received equal attention or carried equal weight. The impoverished rarely wrote newspaper editorials, published tracts, socialized with wealthy community leaders, or occupied prominent political positions. Indeed, the voices of the poor are the hardest to hear in discussions of welfare policy. Poor men and women sometimes testified to their own circumstances and experiences, but their words were usually preserved in the hand of someone else, perhaps a clerk or a relief administrator. Historians looking at almshouse records, for instance, can never be sure what things a needy applicant chose to say or to withhold in order to gain admission. Nor can historians know what a municipal employee chose to write down or to ignore when entering that applicant into the institution's records. Although the poor certainly had their advocates in the debate over public welfare, impoverished women and men themselves produced few written texts that have been preserved in the historical record. One of the challenges in working with the documents in this book, then, is to discern the perspectives of the poor from documents in which their voices are muted, contorted, relayed by proxy, or absent.

Ironically, welfare reform documents published during the early republic may tell us less about the poor and more about the successful Americans who edited newspapers, administered relief programs, served as judges, lawyers, and town leaders, and possessed the power to shape both public policy and discourse. No single motive inspired them to investigate the welfare system. Many were legitimately concerned with the well-being of their fellow human beings and acted from motives of charity and obligation. But these same men and women could simultaneously express a desire to discipline a dangerous class, to minimize government involvement in the labor market, or to solidify their own social prominence through public benevolence.

The alarming "discovery" of poverty in the early republic provided an outlet for ideas about class, status, citizenship, gender, and race. The condemnation, voyeurism, and paranoia that dominated so many official texts—whether the descriptions of impoverished teenagers as "savages" or of poor neighborhoods as "haunts of misery"—reflected assumptions about the larger social order. For historians, it is not enough to simply identify the authors of such treatises as biased. Taking bias as a given (all authors write from a particular point of view), a historian might find important clues in the use of loaded language or a graphic image. Terms like *improvident, debauched,* and *idle* alert us to the preoccupations and self-definition of those Americans spearheading reform efforts.[3]

Welfare reform emerged from what historian Steven Mintz has called "the specter of social breakdown." Poverty triggered larger anxieties about the demise of patriarchal authority, the threat of racial disorder, and the consequences of unfettered economic competition. Moreover, poverty ran counter to the self-image of the new nation and threatened its fragile political experiment.[4] As we shall see, however, Americans of every class would meet these challenges with an uncanny, if unfounded, optimism in the coming decades.

POOR RELIEF IN EARLY AMERICA

Public poor relief was not an invention of the twentieth-century "welfare state." In fact, the United States inherited a system of caring for its poor that dated to fourteenth-century England. As most people led their entire lives in the same place, the system relied on community leaders to assess the need and worthiness of those seeking relief. Anyone taking to the roads in search of more generous aid in a neighboring parish faced arrest and punishment as a vagrant. The laws in American colonies sustained English practices of assigning local responsibility, requiring residency for relief, and enforcing criminal sanctions against the transient poor. Family members, neighbors, church brethren, and philanthropic organizations offered important assistance, but local and state governments administered a network of relief services that ultimately kept most poverty-stricken Americans from perishing in the streets. It would be a mistake to imagine some moment in the national past when the private efforts of kin, clergy, and charities alone fulfilled the needs of impoverished Americans.

Two important considerations organized poor relief in the eighteenth and nineteenth centuries. First, who footed the bill—private groups like churches and benevolent organizations, or state and local governments relying on tax revenue to fund relief programs? Second, what demands were placed upon relief recipients? Would they be assisted in their own homes with supplemental income and supplies, or would they need to enter institutions where their daily activities would be regulated? The answers to these questions can be found in the configuration of early American relief practices, which included outdoor, indoor, private, and public relief programs.

Outdoor relief, or out-relief, consisted of direct aid in the form of food, fuel, clothing, or cash. Recipients of outdoor relief chose for themselves where to live and how to spend their days. Local governments paid "pensions" to men and women with a claim on the community, while numerous private charities offered aid to specific clienteles like sailors' orphans, clergymen's widows, or French immigrants, to name only a few. Outdoor relief almost never provided enough to live on, but an impoverished family might supplement its monthly wages with a few dollars from the city, a load of firewood from a church, and food supplies from a benevolent women's association.

Indoor relief required recipients to leave their homes and enter a regulated facility, such as an almshouse, an asylum, or a house of industry. Smaller communities often gathered five or six elderly or disabled people together under the same roof and expected them to function as a household. Larger cities and towns, however, erected almshouses to hold hundreds at a time and carefully monitored the activities of inmates. Benevolent groups often opened asylums, charity schools, and orphanages as residences for poor children.

Private relief, or charity, entailed the efforts of individuals, churches, or philanthropic organizations. Three benevolent groups in Philadelphia suggest the range of private relief: The Indigent Widows and Single Women's Society raised funds to assist those who met its specific criteria; the Provident Society for the Employment of the Poor procured a building and a great deal of fabric for impoverished women to sew in exchange for monetary aid; and the Association for the Care of Coloured Orphans built an asylum for African American children whose parents were deceased or too impoverished to care for them. Private efforts encompassed both indoor and outdoor relief.

Public relief came from state and local governments, was funded with tax dollars, and aided longtime community residents and the dependents of deceased taxpayers or absent providers. In addition to offering food and money, governments built institutions like almshouses to house the poor collectively. Localities were responsible for their own poor and denied assistance to those without established ties to the community. Impoverished men and women searched for ways around the residency requirement, and as a Baltimore almshouse administrator sarcastically noted, "What they lack in industry, they make up in their ability to tell a good story if it might get them relief."[5]

In practice, the boundaries of public/private and indoor/outdoor were permeable. Most commonly, public officials arranged for the elderly, disabled, and orphaned to receive care in a private household at the taxpayer's expense. Competition was sometimes so great to house a disabled widow or a one-legged sailor that officials held auctions to find the bidder who would accept the lowest payment. Such practices did not augur well for the quality of care, but "pauper auctions" remained common in rural areas well into the nineteenth century. Officials also had little difficulty placing poor children into other households as apprentices. These legal arrangements were not merely a form of foster parenting, but also an essential source of labor for the early republic economy. In exchange for service until the child reached majority age, masters and mistresses offered room and board, literacy education, training in a craft skill, and moral guidance. Parents who brought their children to almshouses regularly forfeited their custody and watched helplessly as their sons and daughters were assigned to new guardians. For children who gained useful job training in artisan households, however, apprenticeships offered a route to economic success in adulthood.

This functional system of relief programs offered a flexible response to need and safeguards against social disorder. It went without saying that poverty was humanity's lot. There was nothing urgent about the fact that many people were poor, and certainly no one harbored expectations of eliminating poverty. The best that could be hoped for was to ease the suffering of the poor without jeopardizing the underpinnings of a well-ordered hierarchical society. Not surprisingly, the American Revolution forced a reevaluation of these assumptions.

THE GROWING PROBLEM OF POVERTY AND ITS VICTIMS

The American Revolution changed the meaning of social inequality and made poverty threatening to the future of the nation. Thinkers like Thomas Jefferson feared that desperate populations of impoverished laborers would collect in American cities and would undermine the political order. As he noted ironically, "The mobs of great cities add just so much to the support of pure government, as sores do to

the strength of the human body."[6] Just as these anxieties were inten-
sifying, changes in the American economy increased the number of
urban workers and the extent to which their livelihoods depended on
inadequate wages. In many regards, early republic welfare reform
marked an effort to reconcile the political inheritance of the American
Revolution with the new social realities of capitalism.

As a republic—a nation where citizens voluntarily adhered to laws
they themselves participated in making—the social order could not
withstand massive inequalities of wealth or the emergence of a dispossessed, but enfranchised, working class. Republics required a roughly
level social structure, where most families could gain access to land
and ultimately support themselves by their own labor. Self-sufficient
families helped meet the second requirement of a republican government: independent citizens who considered their obligations to the
state to be greater than their obligations to landlords, creditors, and
employers. Republican citizens could only be adult, white, male heads
of households because by law women, children, Native Americans,
and African Americans were dependent upon them. Whereas the
dependence of wives, children, and slaves attested to a well-ordered
society, the nation stood imperiled when too many adult white men
rented land instead of owning it, paid interest on debts, labored for
wages, or relied on the government to feed their families.

A successful republic linked its social structure (rough equality) to
the character of its people (independent citizens) to its political institutions. The state needed enough power to maintain public order, but
not so much power that it trampled the rights of citizens. If the social
structure became radically unequal and the citizenry lost its independence, impassioned voters and unscrupulous leaders would usurp governmental power and would redistribute wealth from the few to the
many. This was how previous republics had met their demise, and history offered an irrefutable lesson to the new United States. Of course,
"republican ideology" offered only a theory of how nations rose and
fell, but it was compelling enough to influence the American response
to poverty well into the nineteenth century.

The political thinkers of the Revolutionary era perceived threats to
the new nation at every turn. Urban poverty caused them particular
alarm, for it was the characteristic of a society in decline. Large cities
containing masses of idle paupers suggested the excesses and inequalities that felled earlier republics and made life in the Old World undesirable. Working people must, of course, face a reasonable amount of
want to spur them to industry. As long as the society also provided

ample rewards for that industry, everyone benefitted—a fact to which American agricultural productivity and manufacturing prowess attested. Too much economic success, though, might dangerously accelerate a society's decline. After all, industrial development in England had witnessed the consolidation of wealth into fewer hands and the creation of a landless, dependent population possessing only its labor power to exchange for wages. For a number of republican thinkers like Thomas Jefferson, the trick was to keep the new United States economically vital and productive without following the English path to degeneracy. Jefferson considered the Louisiana Purchase an antidote, as abundant lands would reward industrious farming and small-scale production while delaying the arrival of dispossessed urban laborers.

Although the new United States would remain an agrarian society for its first century of existence, changes were afoot in the early republic that accelerated the arrival of industrial capitalism. An improved transportation infrastructure facilitated the movement of goods across great distances. The new availability of goods, coupled with the proliferation of cash as a medium of exchange, linked urban and rural Americans in a common consumer culture. Farmers, artisans, and manufacturers increasingly made production decisions with an eye toward market exchange. They reconfigured productive processes to gain better efficiencies and to lower labor costs. To produce standardized goods for distant consumption, employers paid wages to workers who had not undergone craft apprenticeships and whose labor entailed less skill and more stamina. The state assisted in creating larger business entities by chartering banks, legalizing complex financial tools, recognizing corporations, and sanctifying property rights in the law. The broader culture legitimated self-interested behavior and celebrated the self-made man who improved his lot through hard work and delayed gratification. Although aspects of capitalism had appeared in Renaissance Venice and Puritan New England, the early republic witnessed the convergence of these practices, ideals, and institutions. Historians have often referred to this moment in American history as the Market Revolution.[7]

Powered by the striving of countless ordinary Americans, the Market Revolution succeeded in spreading the fruits of industry and innovation across the nation. However, as it opened some avenues of economic advancement, it closed others, particularly for urban laborers. An increasing segment of the population now earned scant wages for repetitive and menial labor. Entrepreneurial craftsmen subdivided many artisanal jobs that journeymen and apprentices had previously performed in small workshops. Women, children, and unskilled immigrants performed these "deskilled" tasks for wages far lower than would allow a journeyman to attain his independence. As older paternalistic employment relationships disappeared, journeymen, unskilled immigrant laborers, and women and children competed for many of the same jobs. These workers struggled to convert cash wages into housing, clothing, medical care, and food. Working-class families saw their prospects of homeownership and independence diminish as wages fell behind the cost of living in crowded urban areas.

The unpredictable boom-bust cycle of capitalism added further challenges to the livelihoods of working families. Between 1807 and 1837, a series of shocks sent urban economies tumbling and created massive unemployment and underemployment. The 1807–1809 embargo on European trade imperiled those laborers who were involved in maritime commerce (sailors and porters) or who provided services to mariners entering the port (boardinghouse keepers, laundresses, and prostitutes). The subsequent War of 1812 against Great Britain once again froze commercial traffic in the large port cities and also created a number of war widows who took refuge in public almshouses. The war's end saw the resumption of Atlantic commerce, and American cities were flooded with the inexpensive products of Europe's developing factories and the surplus population of its cities. Several banking scandals dropped the economy into a full-scale panic by 1819. Over the next fifteen years, peaks of recovery and valleys of recession alternated to make economic advancement unreliable for urban workers. The worst would arrive in 1837 when the largest panic yet left thousands of workers scrambling to avoid bankruptcy and the almshouse.

Taking measure of early republic poverty is no easy task. Today, census data and sociological research can tell us the number of Americans living in poverty. However, no agencies recorded such statistics in the early republic, nor did an agreed-upon figure constitute the poverty line. Historians have several options for estimating the extent of poverty in the early republic, but each method assumes different standards of what it meant to be poor: owning too little property to pay taxes, for example, or requiring emergency charity during a cold winter, or relying on governmental support for a sustained period of time.

For example, more than half of Philadelphia households in the 1790s were too poor to pay any taxes if historians take into account the number of male artisans listed as propertyless on assessment lists, the many female-headed households that tax collectors ignored, the numerous boarders and renters who lived under other people's roofs, and the significant population of transients in the city.[8] Those missed by the tax collector were not necessarily needy, but their condition could rapidly decline in the face of cold weather. Baltimore's freezing winter of 1810 sent 10 percent of the city's population to public soup kitchens. Not every worker suffered perilously when cold weather stalled the economy, but many families relied on charity for food and fuel during tough times.[9] The number of urban dwellers dependent on constant relief grew larger through the 1810s and 1820s. In 1830, two thousand New Yorkers spent time in the city's almshouse, while another three thousand families received outdoor relief. Roughly 10 percent of the city's population tapped into the public welfare system.[10]

Such figures are sketchy at best and do not account for families moving in and out of need. These statistics neglect the importance of private charity and ignore the many working families suffering in silence or remaining afloat only by scavenging, begging, and scrimping. But no matter how flawed, these estimates make clear that poverty was no mere figment of the public's imagination.

Of course, not all Americans shared equally in poverty. As is the case today, women were disproportionately poor due to limited occupational choices, inferior wages, and unequal family responsibilities. Coverture, the patriarchal principle that denied women the right to their own property, enforced female dependence—if not upon husbands than upon sources of out-relief. Recognizing the existence of these other forms of support, employers set female wages so low that a full-time job was no guarantee of subsistence. Most women living in poverty were not elderly widows, but rather mothers aged twenty to fifty who lacked support from a male partner.

Recent immigrants were also overwhelmingly poor, having arrived in cities without marketable skills, the capital necessary to purchase land in the west, or a community network to assist them. In particular, Irish Catholic immigrants lacked these resources and quickly found themselves dependent on public relief. During the 1820s, Irish immigrants made up nearly one-quarter of all almshouse inhabitants in Baltimore and New York. Social prejudices against Irish Catholics contributed to immigrants' economic difficulties, while their resulting prominence among the institutionalized poor only reinforced those prejudices.

Discrimination, disfranchisement, and violence left urban free black populations overwhelmingly poor. In northern cities, black residents were excluded from lucrative trades and were denied the ability to defend their property in court. In cities to the south, free African American families devoted their incomes to purchasing relatives out of slavery, making it impossible to accumulate savings. Poverty imposed special burdens on African Americans, such as inferior treatment in almshouses, the likelihood that courts would give custody of their children to white employers, and in parts of the rural South, the right of public officials to sell free black paupers into slavery. Ultimately, the enslavement of several million African Americans dramatically reduced the need for poor relief in much of the country.[11]

RELIGIOUS REFORM AND MORAL BENEVOLENCE

To many early republic Americans, poor relief was less a political question than a religious duty. Alarm over the growth of poverty coincided with a religious effervescence generally known as the Second Great Awakening. From the 1790s through the 1830s, American Protestants revitalized their churches, attracted thousands of converts to spectacular revivals, and espoused the possibility of eradicating sin from the earth. Departing from earlier Calvinist beliefs in predestination and the sinfulness of humanity, religious liberals celebrated free will, self-improvement, and social reform. Evangelicals declared themselves reborn to Christ and harkened a millennium that would arrive not in a fiery apocalypse but once humans cleansed themselves of sin. The belief that humans could *choose* not to sin galvanized Protestants of every kind nationwide and sparked what New England clergyman Lyman Beecher called "the greatest revival of religion that has been since the world began."[12]

Religious zeal translated into social activism. In 1813, Connecticut clergyman Timothy Gillet described "a day of unusual exertions among Christians to do good." Gillet explained, "God is giving all of us an opportunity to be co-workers with him in deeds of benevolence."[13] Christian believers formed an extensive network of voluntary associations—a "Benevolent Empire"—to combat every imaginable social ill. One scholar counted over 1,500 benevolent groups in New England by 1820. "Everything is now done by societies," observed Unitarian Church theologian William Ellery Channing. "You can scarcely name an object for which some institution has not been formed."[14] Indeed, thousands of Americans joined groups to stem prostitution, to curb drinking, to send missionaries to foreign countries, to stop mail delivery on Sunday, to distribute Bibles to nonbelievers, and to relieve the suffering of the poor (to name only a few popular causes). These efforts reflected a perfectionist spirit among devout Christians, who believed that humans could eliminate sin from themselves and sinful practices from society.

Women were at the forefront of organized benevolence. With a tradition of social reform dating to the colonial era, Quaker women in Philadelphia had formed the Female Society for the Relief and Employment of the Poor in 1795. Joining across denominational lines, women in New York, Baltimore, and Charleston started orphan asylums, girls' schools, and charity groups before 1800. As female converts dominated the religious revivalism of the next decades, they also orchestrated church-based charity. Churches in almost every city housed a Dorcas Society, named after the New Testament woman who made clothes for the poor.[15] Although policy-making men and ministers issued the majority of public pronouncements regarding the poor, women spent the most time involved in the day-to-day administration of private charity.

Charity work offered a transformative experience to the elite and middle-class women who made up such groups as Baltimore's Society for the Relief of Distressed Objects or New York's Society for the Relief of Poor Widows with Small Children. In soliciting contributions, visiting poor neighborhoods, and distributing food and fuel, women entered public life and collectively laid claim to privileges and authority denied them individually. Women who were legally unable to own property in their own names controlled thousands of dollars as "directresses" of incorporated charity organizations.

Running the operations of a benevolent group was a full-time job for the women who maintained financial records, wrote public reports, and scheduled home visits to the needy. Moreover, charity work fostered the "bonds of womanhood" among middle-class and elite women. In visiting poor neighborhoods, charitable women gained a greater sense of their own "proper" femininity. While forming an identity in contrast to poor women, elite and middle-class women also saw themselves as similarly dependent on male providers and similarly vulnerable to male vices of drunkenness, abandonment, and infidelity. These realizations propelled benevolent women to assert a greater public authority over private morality and to attempt to regulate respectable male behavior through temperance and antiprostitution societies. Women's rights advocate Lucretia Mott, who began her organizational career relieving the poor, would link women's economic security to their political equality at the 1848 Seneca Falls Convention.[16]

Nonetheless, charitable women were not overly sympathetic to their impoverished sisters. As the wives of merchants and doctors entered rundown neighborhoods to assess the needs of the poor, they brought assumptions about proper gender roles. Their doctrines of domesticity, however, had little applicability in the lives of women who had to leave their homes for labor, who could not depend on a male's protection, and who lacked the leisure time for self-improvement and cultivation of taste. The self-conception of the Albany Society for the Relief of Indigent Women and Children was telling: "Thus, from the overflowing abundance of the rich, are the poor comforted and relieved; while helpless infancy, snatched from ignorance and vice, are now treading cheerfully in the path of virtuous industry." Although the group aided 82 women and schooled 18 children in 1805, most working-class women—in Albany and elsewhere—rejected the cultural authority of their female benefactors and preferred charity unaccompanied by class condescension.[17]

Private charity straddled the line between assisting the poor with their material needs and seeking their moral transformation. Eager to distinguish between deserving and undeserving candidates for relief, benevolent groups injected questions of character into charity. Many charities required recipients to submit to household inspections and to maintain standards of behavior. New York's Society for the Relief of Poor Widows denied aid to women who were seen publicly begging, who refused to bound out their children as apprentices into other households, and who sold liquor from their kitchens. One can only imagine the "improper conduct" that warranted the ejection of ninety-seven-year-old Mrs. McCullum from the rolls of New York's Association for the Relief of Respectable, Aged, and Indigent Females in 1827.[18]

Charity became increasingly linked to moral reform as the millennial implications of religious revivalism took hold. The poor became targets for Christian proselytizers who looked upon poor neighborhoods as "heathen lands" ripe for conversion. Poverty and sin blurred together for groups like the New York Female Missionary Society, which had been founded in 1818 to serve "the poor of this city, who, either on account of their poverty, their wickedness or their ignorance, are destitute of the common ordinances of the Gospel."[19]

The belief that poverty reflected the moral shortcomings of the poor was not new in the early republic. Boston clergyman Charles Chauncy's 1752 sermon, *The Idle-Poor Secluded from the Bread of Charity by the Christian Law,* captured the sentiment of colonial religious leaders and public officials alike. But in the aftermath of the American Revolution and in the midst of the Second Great Awakening, poverty appeared out of place and, ultimately, extinguishable. The "self-made" men and "respectable" women who headed benevolent organizations were inclined to see the poor as responsible for their own misfortune. Explained one Baltimore commentator, "In this country the sober and able-bodied if industriously disposed, cannot long want employment. They cannot, but by their own folly and vices, long remain indigent." In defining its mission, New York's Society for the Prevention of Pauperism (SPP) declared, "Intemperance, ignorance, and idleness are the prolific parents of pauperism." Accordingly, "every exertion should be made to exterminate those dangerous vices, by inculcating religion, morality, sobriety, and industry, and by diffusing useful knowledge among the indigent and laboring people."[20]

The SPP represented a new kind of voluntary association that integrated Christian moral reform and public policy advocacy. Calling to "every person actualized by Christian benevolence, to every good citizen, and to the community at large," the SPP formed committees to study idleness, intemperance, lottery playing, gambling, truancy, and prostitution, among other causes—and effects—of poverty. Despite dwelling on the moral corruption of the poor, the SPP reflected the characteristic optimism of the early republic: Concerned citizens could organize themselves in an extragovernmental capacity, investigate a thorny problem, and cure social ills that had bedeviled other nations throughout history.[21]

When the leading men of Philadelphia or New York organized themselves into committees, descended upon working-class neighborhoods, surveyed officials of relief agencies, and collected their findings in lengthy reports, they publicized startling "discoveries" about the culture of the urban poor. Most disturbingly, alcohol abuse appeared to be the root cause of poverty. The Pennsylvania Society for the Promotion of Public Economy estimated that as many as 90 percent of Philadelphia's poor were chronic drinkers who devoted their wages and whatever charity they received to purchasing alcohol. In the name of stemming poverty, alarmed reformers advocated the strict regulation of taverns and stiff penalties for illegal alcohol vendors. In the reformers' opinion, the moral crisis they uncovered demanded immediate government intervention. "Where our persuasion fails, your coercion should begin," clergyman Abiel Holmes advised civil officials in Cambridge, Massachusetts.[22]

Investigations into the causes of urban poverty brought national attention to alcohol abuse and spawned Temperance, the largest reform movement in the antebellum period. During the first decades of the nineteenth century, men and women consumed staggering quantities of hard liquor on the job, during political assemblages, and in the taverns where they took meals and socialized. One historian calculated that the typical American adult consumed over seven gallons of pure alcohol annually—twice as much as today. No wonder it seems fair to refer to the early United States as "the alcoholic republic." Despite its centrality to American social life, alcohol use had undesirable consequences in the eyes of many: Women identified it as a leading cause of domestic violence; judges resented time wasted on disorderly conduct prosecutions; employers feared lost productivity from employees; anxious Protestants associated it with the boisterous behavior of Irish Catholic immigrants; and of course, public officials blamed it for the rising cost of outdoor relief and the growing population inside almshouses.[23]

Christian moral reformers latched on to alcohol consumption as a sin that human will could—and must—overcome. Massachusetts clergyman Heman Humphrey contended that intemperance stole as many souls as the African slave trade and "sends crowds to hell every year." In 1825, Lyman Beecher delivered six powerful sermons calling alcohol use "unlawful in the sight of God." When the American Temperance Society was formed the following year, the implied moderation of its name was misleading. Over the next decade, one million Americans took pledges of total abstinence from alcohol.[24]

The "benevolent empire" of temperance societies, missionary organizations, and charity groups played a central role in early republic poor relief. Their religious perfectionism made poverty appear curable, but their focus on sin could obscure the structural causes of poverty. It was easier to criticize the poor for squandering their incomes on showy clothing, bawdy theater shows, and lottery tickets than to attribute poverty to the lack of jobs or the inadequacy of wages. Members of New York's SPP or Philadelphia's Union Benevolent Association strove to reshape working-class life in accordance with their own purported values of thrift and self-control, but they had little appreciation for the travails of poor families. Impoverished men and women frequently named "want of employment" as the reason they sought charity, but as one Baltimore moral reformer concluded, the challenge was not to find jobs for the poor, but rather "to fit the poor for employment."[25]

Poverty-stricken Americans were ambivalent toward Christian benevolence. In trying to save souls, moral reformers brought bread, firewood, and clothing that aided their poor households. But impoverished men and women also resented the intrusion of judgmental do-gooders into their homes to scrutinize parenting practices, dietary habits, and cleanliness. A Baltimore pamphleteer considered the tactics of the Society for the Prevention of Pauperism worse than the Spanish Inquisition. In New York, struggling workers suggested that in lieu of "prayers, bibles, and tracts," philanthropists should "afford them the means of an honest living by an honest employment." The working-men's parties and labor unions of the late 1820s and 1830s faulted Christian benevolent organizations for attempting to violate the republican separation of church and state. Urban public officials also remained leery of moral reformers. City councilmen and magistrates did not rush to close the taverns and lottery offices, whose licensing fees provided municipal revenue. Nor did they enforce a police crack-down on working-class neighborhoods, which contained a sizable portion of the voting population and the "houses of ill-fame" that they themselves patronized.[26]

Facing resistance on several fronts and made painfully aware that the number of adult poor was growing despite reform efforts, Christian benevolence turned its attention to impoverished children. Focusing on children made sense in light of the youthfulness of American cities. Children ages fifteen and younger made up one-third of the early republic urban population. "The respectability and happiness of any Country materially depend on the principles and habits of the rising Generation," advised New York Reverend John Stanford. The picture appeared bleak in the cities. "We see our streets crowded with the children of beggars and vagabonds, training up in all the corruption so disgraceful to a christian people," warned a concerned Baltimore citizen. "Save, oh save, from impending ruin the miserable neglected little objects that now infest your streets—take them under your paternal care, and direct their steps in the paths of virtue and honesty," he exhorted his fellow reformers in 1820.[27]

For several decades already, women's benevolent associations had operated charity schools and orphanages for poor girls—or those whom a supporter of the Boston Female Asylum labeled "the most pitiable and most helpless part of the human species." Interest surged among reform-minded women in saving poor children from the fate of their parents. As middle-class households became more reliant upon hired domestic workers, would-be employers worried about bringing irreligious teenaged servants into their homes. Observing a "large number of this class of females growing up from generation to generation in a state not far removed from heathenism," the Female Society of Philadelphia's Second Presbyterian Church opened a girls' school in 1802. "If [servants'] minds were enlarged with the love of truth and rectitude," the founders hoped, "the happiness of hundreds of families might be promoted by it."[28]

Charity schools rarely served more than a few dozen children at a time, leaving many more children without a Christian education. When those children got into trouble, they ended up in almshouses and prisons alongside adult criminals and paupers. Moral reformers called for special juvenile institutions, usually known as "asylums" to connote safety from the dangers of the streets. Although founded by private associations, children's asylums gained official recognition in New York, Philadelphia, Boston, and Baltimore as the ideal repository for juvenile delinquents. When members of the SPP opened the New York House of Refuge in 1825, Reverend Stanford expressed relief that children would no longer graduate from the streets with a "Bachelor in the Art of crime."[29]

In its first four years, the House of Refuge received 527 children from city magistrates. Most had been convicted of vagrancy and petty thefts and would otherwise have been sentenced to the state penitentiary. The institution espoused the modern notion that appeals to "understanding and affection" would bring children to change their behavior. Experience quickly showed otherwise, however, and the facility employed disciplinary means ranging from bed without supper to solitary confinement and restraint in leg irons. Superintendent Nathaniel C. Hart described himself as "too much of the old school" to do without corporal punishment. As Hart said of his charges, "if they are good boys and obey Mr. Hart's rules, he is kind and a father to them, but on the other hand, if they are ugly, lazy, disobedient, and disregard the rules, Mr. Hart is a hard and severe master."[30]

Moral reformers exerted tremendous influence over public-relief policies during the early republic. The same men who served on the boards of Christian charities also held positions in city government or as administrators of almshouses and outdoor relief. Their wives organized church efforts to relieve widows and orphans and conducted visits to impoverished households. In most cities, a small cadre of well-placed men and women carried the moral reform agenda of private charity into the arena of public policy. In both realms, optimism abounded for ending poverty once and for all, but doubts grew whether most poor people themselves were redeemable.

PUBLIC RESPONSIBILITY FOR THE POOR

After visiting almshouses up and down the east coast during the summer of 1835, Boston lawyer Artemas Simonds described a growing consensus on the proper administration of public poor relief. First, "out-door relief should be administered with great care and discrimination," which meant the use of a character test to screen aid recipients. Second, "almshouses should be made comfortable asylums for the really impotent and deserving poor," rather than loosely run repositories of the poor, sick, insane, and criminal. Finally, "the unworthy, the idle, and the vicious . . . should be required to submit to wholesome restraint, labor to the extent of their ability, and live no better than the poor laborer and feeble widow who never ask for public aid." These three principles constituted the agenda of early republic welfare reform and animated virtually every effort to reconfigure public relief policies from 1800 onward.[31]

The origins of this consensus were both material and ideological. In absolute terms, poverty appeared to be getting worse in every city. Almshouse populations and pension lists grew annually, and so too did the number of men, women, and children who begged in the streets. People in real distress—beset by hunger, malnutrition, and exposure—became common sights in the seaport cities, despite the proliferation of private charity and exorbitant municipal expenditures. Elected officials, relief administrators, and private philanthropists (oftentimes one and the same) became convinced that something was amiss.

The rhetoric of moral reform offered one explanation: The poor were themselves to blame. Decrying the sinfulness of American society, moral reformers created a powerful stereotype of the typical relief recipient. He or she was inherently lazy, sexually immoral, and a parasite upon hardworking taxpayers. Suspicion of the poor was not invented in the nineteenth century, but the stridency of the attack reflected the new religious imperative to eradicate vice. It also became easier for prosperous urban residents to criticize the poor because they were increasingly strangers to one another. Whereas rich and poor rubbed elbows in the mixed neighborhoods of colonial-era cities, the early republic witnessed the emergence of working-class districts like the infamous New York slum, Five Points. Residential segregation made it easier to depict the poor as different and defective. As moral reformers circulated their reports of urban vice throughout the country, rural Americans were confirmed in their antipathy toward cities and their inhabitants.

Moral reformers were not the only ones changing the discourse on poverty. At the end of the eighteenth century, political economists began to formulate new understandings of market capitalism. In England, Thomas Malthus and David Ricardo argued grimly that workers would always be mired in poverty. Malthus gained particular notoriety for linking poor relief to overpopulation, famine, war, and disease. Although most American economists remained optimistic that abundant western lands would stave off these dire consequences, scholars like Thomas Cooper, Theodore Sedgwick, and Henry Carey helped enshrine the idea that invisible market forces determined economic success and set the rate of wages at a "natural" level. Government relief could appear as a dangerous interference in the labor market. As political economists celebrated the competitive marketplace, public officials gained a new language for discussing the causes of poverty and the risks of traditional poor-relief policies.[32]

Another set of ideas influenced the welfare reform consensus: a belief in rehabilitative institutions to discipline and reform the deviant. Relief officials drew inspiration from the penitentiary. Incarcerating criminals for long periods of time in hope of effecting their reformation was a novel concept in the late eighteenth and early nineteenth centuries. But the Enlightenment faith in human improvement suggested that isolation, quiet, and total surveillance were more potent than traditional physical punishments like whippings and branding. If penitentiaries could turn convicts into lawful citizens, then so too could a well-regulated almshouse make the poor self-reliant. Older almshouses simply housed the poor, but newer ones would operate as "schools of industry."[33]

Once welfare reform advocates had developed a rationale for new policies, implementation presented additional challenges. Abandoning all public responsibility for the poor was never a goal. As Baltimore almshouse trustee Thomas Griffith observed, "The only difference of opinion which can be tolerated among enlightened men relate merely to the manner of relief."[34] Their fundamental quandary, as historian Michael Katz has explained, was "how to keep the genuinely needy from starving without breeding a class of paupers who chose to live off public and private bounty rather than to work."[35]

The crucial first step was to determine who was deserving of public relief and who was not. Private groups like the Society for the Prevention of Pauperism in New York or the Pennsylvania Society for the Promotion of Public Economy had begun this process in the 1810s. During the following decade, state governments commissioned studies of their own. Massachusetts legislator Josiah Quincy divided the poor into the "impotent" and the "able-bodied." New York Secretary of State Robert Yates proposed the permanent and the temporary poor. In New Hampshire, Reverend Charles Burroughs differentiated the "poor" who were impoverished through no fault of their own and "paupers" who only had themselves to blame. Unitarian minister Joseph Tuckerman suggested the "occasionally and partially" poor, the "frequently and considerably" poor, and the "constantly and absolutely" poor.[36] These malleable categories suggest the difficulty of establishing an absolute standard for relief eligibility.

Tightening access to public relief was of little use, many reformers argued, if sources of private charity remained abundant. Ironically, some reformers believed that the expansion of benevolence in the early republic had become part of the problem: "Increase your charities, augment your gifts, and you add fuel to the fire," warned Heman Humphrey in 1818. A Baltimore newspaper editor accused almsgivers of encouraging beggars' "low, sordid, selfish, and criminal appetites." A plan to force Baltimore's poor into a house of industry would require "a solemn agreement, on the part of the citizens, to withhold, after a specified day, all those contributions which have heretofore tended to encourage idleness and beggary."[37]

As they narrowed avenues to outdoor relief, governments erected larger almshouses to comfort the deserving and punish imposers. When completed in 1816, New York's Bellevue almshouse was the largest structure in the city. Whereas New York's paupers had previously been housed within a stone's throw from city hall, the new almshouse placed the institutionalized poor beyond the city limits. Moreover, Bellevue sported an eleven-foot wall on three sides and the East River on the fourth. The institution isolated the poor from the larger community to facilitate their speedier rehabilitation. Other cities followed suit: Baltimore removed its new almshouse to the countryside, while Newport, Rhode Island, put its facility on an island. These institutions also hired experienced administrators, demanded strenuous labor from inmates, and segregated them by character, age, color, and sex. That way, hardened vagrants could not corrupt innocent widows and children.[38]

In categorizing the poor, limiting access to any kind of out-relief, and building prisonlike almshouses, advocates of welfare reform acted on a very precise logic: By curtailing direct aid, those desiring to live at the public's expense would have to enter an almshouse. But if conditions within the almshouse were made more punitive, people would think twice before subjecting themselves to the austere regimentation of institutional living. Stuck between a rock and a hard place, the undeserving poor would have to clean themselves up and get paying jobs. This set of principles was known as "less-eligibility," meaning that the life of someone on relief should not be more desirable (eligible) than that of someone attempting to eke out an existence solely through industrious labor.

The principle of less-eligibility did not easily translate into policy during the early republic. No comprehensive legislation made this the law of the land, as was the case in Great Britain. In its 1834 Poor Law, Parliament implemented a national welfare system by dividing England and Wales into districts, establishing workhouses in each district, and making all relief dependent upon entering the institution. Such a sweeping action was unlikely in the United States, where no one could imagine the federal government intruding upon such local prerogatives. For this reason, welfare reform in the United States was piecemeal and haphazard.

Philadelphia made the most striking attempt of any city to end outdoor relief. Philadelphia was spending far more on out-relief than any other city, and its generosity made the city a magnet for paupers, who then drove expenditures even higher. In 1828, the city began phasing out cash payments over seven years, intended to coincide with the construction of a massive new almshouse. When the institution was completed, all public relief in Philadelphia would be indoor. But during the intervening seven years, prominent citizens drew attention to the plight of the working poor, particularly female seamstresses whose wages were too low for self-support. Public officials offered an increasing number of exemptions from mandatory institutionalization, and in 1839, the city returned to a mixed system of full-time pensioners on out-relief and a rotating population sheltered at the almshouse. Less-eligibility proved impossible to enforce if the wages of a full-time job still left working families mired in poverty.[39]

Baltimore had never supported many pensioners, but its almshouse became the envy of relief administrators across the nation. After building a new facility far from the city in 1823, Baltimore forced each inmate to labor in exchange for room and board. Administrators offered exemptions to the feeble, but any able-bodied pauper who "eloped" before discharging his or her debt faced arrest and an additional term of penal labor. Residents of the Baltimore almshouse constructed beds and cribs for the facility, laundered sheets and uniforms, and milked cows and grew vegetables on the grounds. The institution never became self-supporting, but it did significantly cut its expenses. "A rigid, uniform system towards paupers, like that of Baltimore," observed an impressed Artemas Simonds, "has the effect either of driving the idle, dissolute, vagrant class to other places, or of compelling them to reform their course in life."[40]

In every city, officials struggled to reconcile the harsh imperatives of welfare reform with civil liberties. American readers knew of Count

Rumford, who used the Bavarian army to round up and institutionalize every pauper in Munich in a single day. Arresting the poor outright was not an option in the United States, despite the sentiment among some that paupers were unfit "to enjoy the blessings of liberty" and "better in a state of confinement, than when they are suffered to run at large."[41] Although every state had a vagrancy statute that essentially criminalized the condition of being homeless, unemployed, or disconnected from a stable community or household,[42] enforcement was sporadic and arbitrary. In Philadelphia, African Americans were targeted, while Baltimore sent 143 women to the state penitentiary during the 1810s. Often used against prostitutes in the absence of more specific laws, vagrancy statutes also fell hard upon women who ventured into public for far more innocuous reasons. Poor women who scoured the docks after dark looking for firewood, female peddlers hawking their wares on the streets, and those traveling alone between communities in search of work might face arrest.[43]

When the town leaders of Boston proposed a house of industry in 1821, they saw little tension between individual liberty and the state's power. In fact, the survival of "a republican form of government" depended upon institutionalizing the "idle and vicious." Every republic hinged on "the character and condition of the mass of the community," Boston leaders explained. "Whatever tends to contaminate, to corrupt, or to demoralize the mass, has a direct effect, not only on the happiness and prosperity of the state, but also on its safety; on the security of property, of life, and of liberty; all of which are, in a republic, directly dependent upon the moral condition and character of the people."[44] Yet it was also possible to argue the opposite position. State institutions, noted a Baltimore critic, would ruin the "spirit of thinking & acting for themselves, which has made our people free and independent, & should keep them so."[45]

Ultimately, the most lasting policy reforms were mundane, involving issues of jurisdiction and finance. Residency requirements remained in place for public relief, and towns often sued one another over responsibility for a given pauper, spending considerable sums transporting poor men and women back to their original residences. Enforcing residency requirements was a losing battle, especially once impoverished European immigrants began arriving en masse in American cities. The New Poor Law in Great Britain had allowed parishes to export their poor, and desperate English paupers soon landed in the United States. Cities attempted to force ship captains to pay a head tax on immigrants or to post a bond covering the expense of housing new arrivals in the almshouse, but crafty captains discharged their passengers outside city limits, and worse, many English paupers snuck into the United States from Canada. New York City officials pleaded for the state government to intervene before the city was "devoured by swarms of people with who she has no alliance, either local or moral." When Ireland's poor came in great numbers in the 1840s, such anxiety became more pronounced and injected virulent nativism into the discussion of public poor relief.[46]

Even before the panic of 1837, many Americans had come to believe once again that some members of society were destined to be poor. Although the economic downturn should have made it easier to view the poor as collectively displaced by uncontrollable economic forces, reformers chose to discuss—albeit with greater resignation—poverty as a matter of individual failure. It was left up to the poor themselves to emphasize the structural causes of their distress and to propose political solutions to inequality.

STRUCTURAL SOLUTIONS FOR POVERTY

Moral reformers in the early republic offered Christian uplift as a cure for poverty, while policymakers proposed larger almshouses and tighter screening of aid recipients. Neither of these approaches generated much enthusiasm among the poor. Of course, impoverished seamstresses, out-of-work sailors, and elderly widows had not been invited to sit on the committees investigating pauperism. Nor did they have the leisure to participate in benevolent organizations. But despite their absence from these levels of the welfare reform debate, the poor were not passive objects of government policy and private charity.

First, by making their own poverty visible—by scavenging for wood on the docks, by begging in the streets, by lining up for every job no matter how low the wages—poor men and women convinced several prominent philanthropists of structural shortcomings in the capitalist economy. Most influentially, Philadelphia publisher Mathew Carey proclaimed, "THE LOW RATE OF WAGES IS THE ROOT OF THE MISCHIEF." In 1829, Carey began a forerunner of present-day living-wage campaigns and sidetracked Philadelphia's efforts to end out-relief. Carey faulted employers who would "grind the faces of the poor" with starvation wages, women's charities that provided work to unemployed seamstresses at even lower rates, and "cold blooded political economists" who justified poverty as the inevitable result of unchallengeable market forces. Carey also lamented pay inequalities that saw women "not averaging, in many cases, more than one third of what is earned by men for analogous employments."[47]

Other philanthropists took the material needs of the poor seriously and formulated concrete plans of assistance. Fuel societies, for example, allowed the poor to invest in firewood during the summer in preparation for the upcoming winter. Soup kitchens frequently aided those needing a meal more than a Bible. Some philanthropists hatched more elaborate plans. In 1834, New England clergyman Charles Burroughs proposed a version of modern Social Security—the government would collect "a small portion of the monthly earnings of each individual, while in years of vigour; exclusively securing it in a savings bank for his own use, and devoting it to his benefit when he shall become infirm, aged, or in adversity"—a century ahead of its time.[48]

In addition to making their material needs known, the poor—and potentially poor—exercised leverage in urban politics. By the 1820s, almost every northern state supported adult white male suffrage, doing away with property requirements for voting. While the most destitute men did not constitute a voting demographic, skilled artisans certainly did. These men considered themselves the "bone and sinew" of society and the guardians of the American Revolution's republican heritage. For generations, the craft economy had offered them a steady path of upward mobility from apprentice to journeyman to self-employment as a master artisan. But those expectations were dashed by the 1820s, as changes in production made it far less likely that journeymen would advance to independence. As some masters built larger workshops and deskilled their labor force, other masters slipped back into journeymen status and became wage earners. And many young journeymen feared that the slightest economic disruption would cast their families on public relief. At the end of the 1820s, militant artisans formed trade unions and political coalitions to protect their interests. They drew attention to poverty as a problem of unjust wealth distribution and unequal opportunity rather than one of personal moral failure.

Turnouts, or strikes, called attention to the inadequacy of wages and showed that female workers, as well as male, could use the strength of numbers to stave off poverty. Sixteen hundred New York "tailoresses" joined together in 1831 to fight for a standardized pay scale. "Long have the poor tailoresses of this city borne this oppression in silence," noted striker Sarah Monroe, "and in my opinion to be longer silent would be a crime." Asked one organizer of the United Tailoresses Society, "If union is strength, why should we be weak?"[49]

"If the working classes were not unjustly deprived of their rights, they would need no charity," declared a correspondent to the *Free Enquirer,* the New York newspaper of Robert Dale Owen and Frances Wright. Owen and Wright advocated the rights of workers and the poor by opposing bankers, monopolists, and ministers. Like other reformers in the early republic, they mixed alarm over the status quo with an optimistic belief in a better future. "The increasing spirit of enquiry will stimulate the producing classes to seek the cause of their own increasing impoverishment," warned the *Free Enquirer,* "and this discovered, there is nothing to hinder them in this country from applying an effectual remedy."[50]

Labor radicals demanded that government serve the interests of common people. At one extreme, Thomas Skidmore hoped to harness the power of the state to equalize property. A machinist who helped start the New York Workingman's Party, Skidmore advocated the abolition of inheritance. Under his plan, the property of those who died in a given year would be redistributed to everyone (male and female, black and white) reaching majority age in that same year. Equally controversial was the plan for state-run boarding schools championed by Owen and Wright. A progressive system of taxation would fund "national, rational, republican education; free for all, at the expense of all; conducted under the guardianship of the state, at the expense of the state, and for the honor, the happiness, the virtue, the salvation of the state." Neither the inheritance plan nor the boarding school plan aroused solid support in working-class communities.[51]

Public education nonetheless remained a rallying point for working-class activists. "Until the means of equal education shall be equally secured to all," noted a Philadelphia workingmen's committee, "liberty is but an unmeaning word, and equality an empty shadow."[52] Like moral reformers, the advocates of common schools invested their hopes in the rising generation. Of course, private benevolent groups had operated charity schools for poor children since the 1790s. However, education was not a matter of charity, but a right, according to working-class newspapers like the *Free Enquirer.* The emergence of public elementary and secondary schools in the 1830s reflected the advocacy of working-class voters and their faith that education was an antidote to poverty.

Workingmen's parties and labor unions pushed for other reforms beneficial to the poor. They rallied for the abolition of debt imprisonment, a practice that allowed private creditors to place delinquent debtors in jail until family members and friends could discharge the obligation. Other important causes included a fair land policy for making western farms available to eastern laborers, a mechanics' lien so that workers could claim overdue wages from bankrupt employers, a ban on prison workshops that undersold artisan workshops, and a ten-hour day to give workers the leisure time to read, engage public issues, and pursue self-improvement. Such demands defined early republic labor politics until the serious economic downturn of 1837 sapped the entire movement. With their members unemployed, labor unions fell apart, and workingmen's parties crumbled. In the following decades, isolated voices continued to critique the capitalist economy and proposed structural solutions to poverty, but in comparison, the late 1820s and 1830s had marked a rare moment of activism by and on behalf of the poor. Although voting for labor candidates or striking for the ten-hour day might seem on face value as unrelated to welfare reform, working-class men and women made a compelling case that increased economic opportunities would go farther than new almshouses to end poverty.

THE LEGACY OF WELFARE REFORM

Poverty and poor relief remained significant concerns in American life after 1837. Reformers like Dorothea Dix publicized atrocious living conditions in almshouses across the country. New York's Association for Improving the Condition of the Poor kept the moral reform tradition alive by sending visitors to poor households and publishing shocking exposés of life in urban slums. Nonetheless, the aspirations of private philanthropists and public officials departed from the optimism of the early republic. Concern for the poor did not disappear in the aftermath of the panic of 1837, but upper- and middle-class Americans perceived urban poverty as entrenched rather than eradicable. Public relief and private charity might treat the symptoms of poverty, but they were unlikely to effect a permanent cure. In most cities, relief programs shrunk as a percentage of municipal budgets, while funding for new police departments rose dramatically.

The best hope for staving off the arrival of an urban proletariat, almost everyone agreed, was public schooling. That education held the key to economic advancement had become a sacred creed for middle-class moralists and working-class Americans alike. Taxpayer-funded, compulsory, nonsectarian public schools appeared during the 1830s and 1840s in state after state. Massachusetts was the first to assume state responsibility for universal public education. Horace Mann, secretary of the state's board of education, called public schools a "great equalizer." In the charity schools and private academies of the earlier period, rich and poor children remained segregated, but in public schools, all children mingled together in the democratic spirit of the age. Proper education was essential, offered Mann, in a republican society in which the ignorant were not prevented from voting. Because educational reformers like Mann expressed fears of class conflict and disorder, it is not difficult to portray public education as a sinister mechanism of social control. Although public schools did serve a disciplinary function, they also opened new avenues to upward mobility for the urban poor.[53]

As the nation's attention turned to slavery in the decades before the Civil War, the issue of public welfare punctuated the arguments of northern abolitionists and southern slaveowners. As early as the 1830s, the defenders of slavery began noting the absence of paupers in their communities relative to the extensive poverty in northern cities. The *Southern Literary Messenger* advised abolitionists to "look at home" for more pressing social ills. "They will perhaps find enough to do in mitigating the wretchedness of their *white* brethren." Southern ideologues would describe slavery as the ultimate form of public welfare: cradle-to-grave support for the working class. "In all the elements of physical comfort, and in the facilities of mental cultivation and moral improvement," continued the *Literary Messenger,* slaves "possess immeasurable advantages over the same class of population in this or any other country under the broad canopy of heaven." A Southern doctor visiting New York in 1832 claimed that the city's poor were "far more filthy, degraded, and wretched than any slave I have ever beheld, under the most cruel and tyrannical master."[54]

The early republic discussion of poor relief actually generated ammunition for slavery's defenders. Decrying female poverty, Presbyterian minister Ezra Stiles Ely reported that "a common slave" earned a better living than a seamstress in New York City. "Wage slavery" became a rallying point for working-class activists in the north. Their low pay made them like slaves, as did their poverty once cities began forcing relief recipients to labor in almshouses. The *Free Enquirer* called upon officials to consider "whether this compelling to work, or starve" made them worse than "a slave in the field of a southern planter." Almshouse labor struck a jarring chord in Southern communities like Baltimore or Charleston, where the implications of personal freedom (or the lack thereof) were so obvious. White paupers were unlikely to gain an appreciation for labor when every other message in society denigrated work as the lot of the enslaved.[55]

By raising important questions about work—who must perform it, on what terms, and under what controls—the early republic welfare reform debate invariably juxtaposed wage labor and slavery and helped northerners and southerners to enunciate sectional differences in the coming decades.[56] White southerners reaffirmed their commitment to slavery, describing it as a "positive good" from the 1830s onward. All societies relied on exploited labor, southern ideologues like James Henry Hammond and George Fitzhugh would argue. At least, slavery placed the burden on an "inferior race" rather than upon white citizens. In contrast, northerners became increasingly convinced of slavery's evils. With slavery as a foil, the wage system—once a danger to republican governance and a degraded form of labor—gained acceptance in the north. Although working-class poverty became more prevalent, northern leaders became less concerned in the 1840s and 1850s because southern slavery posed a greater threat to the nation's health. The conflict between northern free-labor and southern proslavery ideology would soon overshadow the urgency that men and women from Boston to Baltimore brought to welfare reform in the early republic.

A NOTE ABOUT THE TEXT

Original spellings and punctuation are maintained throughout the documents in this volume. In the interest of clarity, however, the traditional early American long "s" (*f*) has been modernized. Brackets [] and numbered footnotes contain editorial clarifications. Ellipses (...) indicate that parts of the original texts have been omitted for reasons of space. Many of the documents in this volume are excerpts from longer works, but the included selections fully convey the flavor, meaning, and argument of the original texts. The decision to include smaller portions of longer texts serves to highlight the diversity of early republic thought within the space of this small book. Students undertaking further research should consult the original texts.

NOTES

[1] Mathew Carey, *Address to the Wealthy of the Land . . .* (Philadelphia: Wm. F. Geddes, 1831), 27. Although urban poverty garnered the most attention, rural poverty was prevalent; Steven Sarson, "'Objects of Distress': Inequality and Poverty in Early Nineteenth-Century Prince George's County," *Maryland Historical Magazine* 96 (summer 2001): 141–62.

[2] "Circular. To the Select-Men of the Town of Guilford," New-York Historical Society Library [NYHS], broadside collection, 1820:33.

[3] The editors of a recent collection of English texts on poverty and welfare have labeled them "semi-factual." See John Marriott and Masaie Matsumura, eds., *The Metropolitan Poor: Semi-Factual Accounts, 1795–1910*, 6 vols. (London: Pickering and Chatto, 1999).

[4] Steven Mintz, *Moralists and Modernizers: America's Pre–Civil War Reformers* (Baltimore: Johns Hopkins University Press, 1995), 3–15.

[5] Ruth Wallis Herdon, *Unwanted Americans: Living on the Margin in Early New England* (Philadelphia: University of Pennsylvania Press, 2001), 1–10; J. Cushing to the Second Branch of the City Council, Jan. 25, 1834, Baltimore City Archives [BCA], RG 16, s 1, box 49.

[6] Thomas Jefferson, *Notes on the State of Virginia*, Query 19.

[7] Paul Gilje, ed., *Wages of Independence: Capitalism in the Early American Republic* (Madison, Wisc.: Madison House Publishers, 1997); Paul E. Johnson, "The Market Revolution," in Mary K. Cayton et al., eds., *Encyclopedia of American Social History* (New York: Charles Scribner's Sons, 1993), 1:545–60; Charles Sellers, *The Market Revolution: Jacksonian America, 1815–1846* (New York: Oxford University Press, 1991).

[8] Billy G. Smith, "The Vicissitudes of Fortune: The Careers of Laboring Men in Philadelphia, 1750–1800," in Stephen Innes, ed., *Work and Labor in Early America* (Chapel Hill: University of North Carolina Press, 1988), 225–33; Richard Oestreicher, "The Counted and the Uncounted: The Occupational Structure of Early American Cities," *Journal of Social History* 28 (winter 1994): 351–61.

[9] "The Distributors Met at the Council Chamber, February 24, 1810," BCA, RG 41, s 1, box 4; *Baltimore American,* Feb. 17 and 24, 1817.

[10] Boston Common Council, *Report on Almshouses and Pauperism* (Boston: J. H. Eastburn, 1835), 54.

[11] James D. Watkinson, "'Fit Objects of Charity': Community, Race, Faith, and Welfare in Antebellum Lancaster County, Virginia, 1817–1860," *Journal of the Early Republic* 21 (spring 2001): 57.

[12] Mintz, *Moralists and Modernizers,* 16–29; Louis Masur, *1831: Year of Eclipse* (New York: Hill and Wang, 2001), 64 (Beecher quote).

[13] Timothy Phelps Gillet, *Charity Profitable; or God a Surety for the Poor: A Sermon, Delivered before the Female Charitable Society, in Guilford, January 6, 1813* (New Haven: Oliver Steele, 1813), 12–13.

[14] William Ellery Channing, as quoted in Conrad E. Wright, *The Transformation of Charity in Post-Revolutionary New England* (Boston: Northeastern University Press, 1992), 5, 182.

[15] Acts 9:36–43.

[16] Lori Ginzberg, *Women in Antebellum Reform* (Wheeling, Ill.: Harlan Davidson, 2000), 15–28; Suzanne Lebsock, *The Free Women of Petersburg: Status and Culture in a Southern Town, 1784–1860* (New York: W. W. Norton, 1984), 195–205; Nancy F. Cott, *The Bonds of Womanhood: "Women's Sphere" in New England, 1780–1835* (New Haven: Yale University Press, 1977); Margaret Morris Haviland, "Beyond Women's Sphere: Young Quaker Women and the Veil of Charity in Philadelphia, 1790–1810," *William and Mary Quarterly* 51 (July 1994): 419–46.

[17]*A Brief Account of the Society Established in the City of Albany for the Relief of Indigent Women and Children* (Albany: Charles R. and George Webster, 1805), 4. Christine Stansell details the tension between women of different classes in *City of Women: Sex and Class in New York, 1789–1860* (New York: Alfred A. Knopf, 1986).

[18]*The By-Laws and Regulations of the Society for the Relief of Poor Women with Small Children . . .* (New York: J. Seymour, 1813), 6–8, 18; Association for the Relief of Respectable, Aged, and Indigent Females in New York City, NYHS, misc. mss.

[19]*Second Anniversary Report, of the Female Missionary Society for the Poor of the City of New-York, and Its Vicinity* (New York: Gould, 1818), 7.

[20]*To the Citizens of Baltimore* (Baltimore: T. Maund, 1822); *Documents Relative to Savings Banks, Intemperance, and Lotteries . . .* (New York: E. Conrad, 1819), 21.

[21]*First Annual Report of the Managers of the Society for the Prevention of Pauperism in the City of New-York . . .* (New York: J. Seymour, 1818), 6.

[22]*Report of the Library Committee of the Pennsylvania Society for the Promotion of Public Economy* (Philadelphia: Merritt, 1817), 17; Abiel Holmes, *A Discourse, Delivered at the Opening of the New Almshouse in Cambridge* (Cambridge, Mass.: Hilliard and Metcalf, 1818), 23.

[23]W. J. Rorabaugh, *The Alcoholic Republic: An American Tradition* (New York: Oxford University Press, 1979); Ronald Walters, *American Reformers, 1815–1860,* rev. ed. (New York: Hill and Wang, 1997), 125–46.

[24]Heman Humphrey, *On Doing Good to the Poor: A Sermon . . .* (Pittsfield, Mass.: Phinehas Allen, 1818), 14; Heman Humphrey, *Parallel between Intemperance and the Slave Trade: An Address Delivered at Amherst College, July 4, 1828* (Amherst, Mass.: J. S. and C. Adams, 1828); Lyman Beecher, *Six Sermons on the Nature, Occasions, Signs, Evils, and Remedy of Intemperance* (New York: American Tract Society, 1827), 103.

[25]*To the Citizens of Baltimore.*

[26]*A Warning to the Citizens of Baltimore* (Baltimore: n.p., 1821); Masur, *1831,* 80.

[27]"Howard," *Baltimore American,* Feb. 2, 1820; John Stanford to the Mayor of New York, Jan. 21, 1812, NYHS, misc. mss., Stanford Papers, box 2.

[28]Thaddeus M. Harris, *A Discourse Preached before the Members of the Boston Female Asylum* (Boston: Russell, Cutler, 1813); Female Society of the Second Presbyterian Church in Philadelphia to Reverend Philip Milledoler, Nov. 9, 1802, NYHS, misc. mss., Milledoler Papers.

[29]John Stanford, *A Discourse on Opening the New Building in the House of Refuge, New-York . . .* (New York: Mahlon Day, 1826), 12.

[30]*Second Annual Report of the Managers of the Society for the Reformation of Juvenile Delinquents in the City of New-York* (New York: Mahlon Day, 1827), 6–8, 58; N. C. Hart to Stephen Allen, Dec. 17, 1834, NYHS, misc. mss., Stephen Allen Papers. See also Robert S. Pickett, *House of Refuge: Origins of Juvenile Reform in New York State, 1815–1857* (Syracuse, N.Y.: Syracuse University Press, 1969).

[31]Boston Common Council, *Report on Almshouses,* 44; Josiah Quincy, *Report of the Committee on the Pauper Laws of This Commonwealth* [1821], and John Yates, *Report of the Secretary of State in 1824 on the Relief and Settlement of the Poor,* reprinted in David Rothman, ed., *The Almshouse Experience: Collected Reports* (New York: Arno Press, 1971); *Report Concerning the Pauper Laws of New Hampshire, to the Honorable, the Senate and House of Representatives* (Concord, N.H.: n.p., 1821); *Report of the Commissioners Appointed by an Order of the House of Representatives, Feb. 29, 1832, on the Subject of the Pauper System of the Commonwealth of Massachusetts* (Boston: Dutton and Wentworth, 1833).

[32]Robert Heilbroner, *The Worldly Philosophers: The Lives, Times, and Ideas of the Great Economic Thinkers,* 7th ed. (New York: Touchstone, 1999); Paul Conkin, *Prophets of Prosperity: America's First Political Economists* (Bloomington: Indiana University Press, 1980).

[33]David Rothman, *Discovery of the Asylum: Social Order and Disorder in the New Republic* (Boston: Little, Brown, 1971).

[34]Douglas G. Carroll Jr. and Blanche D. Coll, "The Baltimore Almshouse: An Early History," *Maryland Historical Magazine* 66 (summer 1971): 149.

[35]Michael B. Katz, *In the Shadow of the Poorhouse: A Social History of Welfare in America* (New York: Basic Books, 1986), 18. Taking the long view, Katz argues that American welfare reform has been a consistent effort "to define, locate, and purge" the ineligible from public relief rolls.

[36]Quincy, *Report of the Committee on the Pauper Laws,* 4; Yates, *Report of the Secretary of State,* 941; Charles Burroughs, *A Discourse Delivered in the Chapel of the New Alms-House, in Portsmouth, N.H. . . .* (Portsmouth: J. W. Foster, 1835), 9; Joseph Tuckerman, "Who Are the Poor?" in E. E. Hale, ed., *Joseph Tuckerman on the Elevation of the Poor: A Selection of His Reports as Minister at Large in Boston* (1874; reprint, New York: Arno Press, 1971), 63.

[37]Humphrey, *On Doing Good to the Poor,* 20; *Baltimore Morning Chronicle,* Apr. 15, 1820, as quoted in Blanche D. Coll, "The Baltimore Society for the Prevention of Pauperism, 1820–1822," *American Historical Review* 61 (Oct. 1955): 83; House of Industry Papers, 1822, BCA, RG 19, s 9, box 1.

[38]*Report of the Committee Appointed by the Guardians of the Poor of the City and Districts of Philadelphia . . .* (Philadelphia: Samuel Parker, 1827), 13, 21–22; Raymond Mohl, *Poverty in New York, 1783–1825* (New York: Oxford University Press, 1971), 85.

[39]*Report of the Committee Appointed by the Guardians of the Poor,* 30, 24; Priscilla F. Clement, *Welfare and the Poor in the Nineteenth-Century City: Philadelphia, 1800–1854* (Rutherford, N.J.: Fairleigh Dickenson Press, 1985), 72–75.

[40]Boston Common Council, *Report on Almshouses,* 26.

[41]*The Philanthropist: Or, Institutions of Benevolence, by a Pennsylvanian* (Philadelphia: Isaac Peirce, 1813), 37–38.

[42]Because vagrancy statutes criminalize a person's condition, rather than his or her actions, they are somewhat unique within American law. Additionally, they may be applied selectively against a given segment of the population. As Anatole France sarcastically noted in *The Red Lily* (1894): "The law, in its majestic equality, forbids the rich as well as the poor, to sleep under bridges, to beg in the streets, and to steal bread."

[43]Maryland Penitentiary (Prisoners Record), 1811–1840, Maryland State Archives, s-275; Priscilla F. Clement, "The Transformation of the Wandering Poor in Nineteenth-Century Philadelphia," in Eric H. Monkkonen, ed., *Walking to Work: Tramps in America, 1790–1935* (Lincoln: University of Nebraska Press, 1984), 56–84.

[44][Town of Boston], *Report of the Committee for Erecting a House of Industry, October 22, 1821* (Boston: n.p., 1821), 13.

[45]Thomas W. Griffith to the Mayor and City Council, Feb. 22, 1821, BCA, RG 16, s 1, box 21.

[46]Robert E. Cray, *Paupers and Poor Relief in New York City and Its Rural Environs, 1700–1830* (Philadelphia: Temple University Press, 1988), 182; Clement, "The Transformation of the Wandering Poor," 56–84; Boston Common Council, *Report on Almshouses,* 36; *Second Annual Report of . . . the Society for the Prevention of Pauperism* (New York: E. Conrad, 1820), 21.

[47]Mathew Carey, *Miscellaneous Essays* (Philadelphia: Carey, 1830), 266–87 (quote on 281); *Free Enquirer,* Apr. 10, 1830.

[48]Burroughs, *A Discourse,* 86.

[49]Nancy Cott et al., eds., *Root of Bitterness: Documents of the Social History of American Women,* 2nd ed. (Boston: Northeastern University Press, 1996), 118–22.

[50]*Free Enquirer,* Dec. 19, 1829, Mar. 11, 1829.

[51]See Documents 21 and 22 in this volume. On the education plan, see *Free Enquirer,* Dec. 5, 1829.

[52]*Working Man's Advocate* (N.Y.), Mar. 6, 1830.

[53]Mintz, *Moralists and Modernizers,* 106–112; Sellers, *Market Revolution,* 367–69.

[54]R. T. H., "White and Black Slavery," *Southern Literary Messenger* 6 (Mar. 1, 1840), 194; Tyler Anbinder, *Five Points: The Nineteenth-Century New York City Neighborhood That Invented Tap Dance, Stole Elections, and Became the World's Most Notorious Slum* (New York: Free Press, 2001), 35. See also "Governor McDuffie's Message on the Slavery Question, 1835," in Albert Bushnell Hart and Edward Channing, eds., *American History Leaflets,* no. 10 (New York: Parker P. Simmons, 1909); John C. Calhoun, "Speech on the Reception of Abolition Petitions, February 6, 1837, U.S. Senate," in Eric L. McKitrick, ed., *Slavery Defended: The Views of the Old South* (Englewood Cliffs, N.J.: Prentice-Hall, 1963), 12–19.

[55]*Free Enquirer,* Mar. 11, 1829; David Roediger, *Wages of Whiteness: Race and the Making of the American Working Class* (New York: Verso, 1991), 65–92.

[56]Drew Gilpin Faust, *The Ideology of Slavery: Proslavery Thought in the Antebellum South, 1830–1860* (Baton Rouge: Louisiana State University Press, 1981); Jonathan Glickstein, "Poverty Is Not Slavery: American Abolitionists and the Competitive Labor Market," in Lewis Perry and Michael Fellman, eds., *Antislavery Reconsidered: New Perspectives on the Abolitionists* (Baton Rouge: Louisiana State University Press, 1979), 195–219; Thomas Bender, ed., *The Antislavery Debate: Capitalism and Abolitionism as a Problem in Historical Interpretation* (Berkeley: University of California Press, 1992).

PART TWO

The Documents

Elite Perceptions of Poverty as a Moral and Social Crisis

1

The Pennsylvania Society for the Promotion of Public Economy

1817

The freezing weather of February 1817 impelled Philadelphia's leading citizens to collect funds for the immediate relief of the city's poor. As they organized that effort, they took it upon themselves to investigate the causes of poverty. A select committee of twelve prominent community members addressed eighteen questions to their peers who were engaged in administering poor relief, primarily district managers of public aid programs and officers of private charity groups. More than thirty people responded to the survey, but none were residents of working-class neighborhoods or recipients of public charity; their opinions were absent from the discussion. Provoked by the findings of the survey, leading Philadelphians founded the Pennsylvania Society for the Promotion of Public Economy, which formed new committees to investigate poor laws, prisons, taverns, and public schools. They also republished the initial survey, interspersing the committee's opinion with direct (but unattributed) quotations from various respondents.

Report of the Library Committee of the Pennsylvania Society for the Promotion of Public Economy (Philadelphia: Merritt, 1817).

Query 1. What description of persons are most improvident?

The people of colour; the lower classes of Irish emigrants; the intemperate and day labourers are generally considered as the most improvident.

Query 2. What do the poor allege as the cause of their poverty?

In most instances want of employment is the alleged cause, especially in the winter season, but, although this may temporarily operate, idleness, intemperance, and sickness are most frequently the real causes; to which are added at present, the high prices of provisions and fuel, especially the latter, as it is generally purchased by the poor in small quantities, from the grocery and liquor stores, at a very exorbitant advance upon the prime cost.[1]

"This excuse (want of work) although sometimes feigned, is generally true. The great disproportion which exists between the prices of labour of men and women, is a matter of serious regret; and to restore the equilibrium, by withdrawing men from the occupations and pursuits which women are capable of performing, seems to be worth the attention of the political economist."

Query 3. What proportion of the indigent are widows and single women?

Upon this subject, those reports, which are merely conjectural, disagree very materially, some stating 1-10th others 1-3d 1-4d and 3-4ths.

From the returns of the guardians of the poor it appears that of 1239 paupers, 673 were widows and single women; the latter in very small proportion.

The "society for supplying the poor with soup" state that of 611 adults, 235 were widows, or women whose husbands (if they had any) were absent; there were also 45 women without families, but whether widows or single women, they were not able to determine. . . .

Query 4. Are, or are not, many women abandoned by their husbands and left with families to support; and what are the reasons assigned for such desertion?

Few persons, we presume, are prepared to anticipate the result of this inquiry; the evil is lamentably extensive, and calls loudly for some

---

[1] *advance upon the prime cost:* with a significant retail mark-up in price.

effectual remedy. In almost every report some instances are noticed. The guardians of the poor, alone, enumerate 133 cases of desertion, of which 67 were caused by the intemperance, generally of the husband, but sometimes of the wife. The next most frequent reason for desertion appears to be enlistment in the army during the late war.[2] Other causes are mentioned, such as the want of employment and the expectation of finding it elsewhere; improper connexions formed without reflection or attachment and without the means of supporting a family. Desertions are said to be "particularly frequent amongst the negroes. Among the majority of them the marriage contract appears to be considered a mere civil contract, hardly that. Marriages are frequently made before magistrates, these should be discountenanced. The contract in this case wants a sanction."

Query 5. What proportion of the poor are sick, and what appears or is said to be the cause of the indisposition?

It does not appear, from the information before the committee, that the proportion of sick is very great. The answers to this question generally do not specify numbers. The guardians of the poor enumerate 144 [of 1,239]. The prevailing diseases are rheumatism, consumption and colds, arising chiefly from exposure to inclement weather, in consequence of being miserably accommodated in their dwellings, without a sufficiency of fuel, or of clothing suitable for the season. Several cases are mentioned as proceeding from improper food and from intemperance. . . .

"The mortality of the children of the poor is greatest generally in the summer; it is hardly possible to conceive the impurity of the air at that season in and around the residence of such as live in alleys and obscure places. Many children are doubtless hurried to the grave from this cause alone."

Query 6. What particular trade is most affected in the winter season? and is there, or is there not, unusual suffering experienced by young mechanics who have families to support?

"The trades connected with commerce and building, such as ship carpenter, riggers, caulkers, sail maker, carpenters, plaisterers, bricklayers and their labourers, as also day labourers. Those who navigate the rivers are said to suffer particularly. Young mechanics who have families to

[2]*the late war:* the War of 1812.

support are not believed to be especially exposed to suffering, "unless it be produced by idleness, want of economy and frequenting drinking clubs and societies."

"The various manufactories, whose operations have been suspended, have heretofore furnished employment to a very considerable number of poor, especially to women and children, who have during the past autumn and winter been discharged in consequence of the suspension of business and are thus thrown out of employment. It is stated that some manufacturers have dismissed 50 to 100 hands, and the number thus discharged in the city and neighbourhood is estimated at several thousands."

"I have no doubt there are in this city from seven to ten thousand young and old people, who, if manufacturers were prospering would earn two dollars per week, that are now idle and suffering; they would support themselves respectably and add a vast sum to the amount of the general wealth."

Query 7. Are, or are not, seamen subject to great privations?

The general impression appears to be that they are not, as, if not employed they can generally obtain a credit at boarding houses until an opportunity present of going to sea. The families of those who are at sea, and who have not left monthly orders upon their employers do suffer severely, occasionally, being frequently extravagant, and always improvident. . . .

Query 8. What proportion of the poor are strangers not entitled to legal residence, and if foreigners from what country have they come?

A considerable proportion of the poor are foreigners, some of whom have obtained a legal residence.

Of 1239 pensioners upon the poor list, 540 are natives of other places than the city and liberties.[3] The following statement collected from the returns of the guardians will exhibit from what countries they came.

---

[3] *liberties:* suburbs.

From Ireland	250	Delaware	21
Germany and Holland	84	Pennsylvania	17
Scotland	23	Maryland	3
England	20	New-York	2
Wales	3	New England	3
France	1	Parts of the U. States	
		not specified	14
W. Indies	2		60
New-Jersey	97		
	480		

In 1816, 413 non-resident paupers, were admitted into the Alms-house, and during the same period 1323 paupers made their first entrance into that institution.

From the 1st of January to 28th February, 1817, there were admitted into the Alms-house 468 persons, of whom 87 had no legal residence. The managers assert that the major part of the paupers in that house are foreigners by birth. Those from the neighbouring states generally pass the winter in the city at the public expense, and in the spring return to their homes, where by a little labour they are enabled to support themselves during the summer.

Query 9. What proportion of paupers are descendants of Africa?

It is a popular opinion that the greater part of the poor are descendants of Africa, but this is not supported by the facts derived from the documents. The reports differ very widely relative to the proportion of whites and blacks. From 1-6th to 3-4ths are stated to be blacks. But according to the reports of the guardians of the poor . . . about 18½ per cent for the proportion of the descendants of Africa.[4]

Query 10. Is, or is not, the use of ardent spirits the cause of poverty, and do, or do not, those who receive, expend the means afforded for their subsistence in purchasing that article?

All reports excepting in one or two instances, reply to the former part of this query in the affirmative. The following extracts, written by

---

[4]African Americans made up roughly 11 percent of the city's population in 1817.

different persons, will exhibit at one view the almost universal senti-ment upon this subject.

"We believe the use of ardent spirits is the principal source of poverty, depravity and wretchedness."

"The use of ardent spirits is probably in nine cases out of ten the cause of poverty."

"The use of ardent spirits appears to be the primary cause of the poverty and distress which prevail amongst the lower class, and a large proportion of their earnings, as well as of the sums distributed for their relief is expended in tippling houses."

"It is a melancholy fact that the excessive use of ardent spirits is the cause of poverty, of a very large proportion of those who receive pub-lic charity, probably 2-3ds; and there is no doubt but the alms which are bestowed on such is frequently expended in purchasing this article. We believe more money is expended in the course of a year by the poor for this destructive article than would be sufficient, (if husbanded) to provide for all their wants during an inclement winter."

[Several similar statements omitted.]

Query 11. What proportion of the children of the poor go to school, and how are those employed who do not?

It seems to be the general opinion as far as it can be ascertained from the answers to this question, which are very indefinite, that a very small proportion go to school; the greatest that is mentioned is one third, which however is not confirmed by the following data.

One report states that of 40 children 8 go to school and 10 are bound out at trades and in families.

Another, that of 111 children 17 go to school, 5 are hired out, and the remainder are too young or not mentioned. "Those who do not go to school are engaged in practices injurious to their morals, and laying the foundation of lasting wretchedness by the habits which they acquire."

Query 12. Are, or are not, pawn-brokers instrumental in reducing many persons to want?

Upon this subject there is very little information, but as far as it extends, they are considered as "reducing many to wretchedness and want." Clothes-sellers and lotteries are mentioned under this head in several reports as very great evils. In Southwark,[5] pawn-brokers appear to be numerous. One report from that district says, "they are great nuisances in society by reducing many to penury and wretchedness, and call loudly for their suppression." "The great number of pawn-brokers is a most serious growing evil, and they are certainly instrumental in reducing many persons to want."

To the question as thus stated by the guardians of the poor, "are you acquainted with any cases of extortion or oppression by pawn-brokers? if so, please to state them; also, what do you believe to be the amount of interest per cent which they charge per month?" it is replied,

"Only one, in which he receives one hundred per cent per annum."

"I am acquainted with one case wherein they receive 12½ per cent per month."

"I have known them to charge 12 per cent per month." Three others mention 5 to 18 per cent per month.

"The effects of pawn-brokers cannot from their nature be otherwise than pernicious; they are only resorted to in cases of great distress, and in but few instances are the poor, we presume, able to redeem their goods, deposited for an advance very disproportionate to their value."

Query 13. What portion of the poor are willing to labour if they could obtain work all the year? And does, or does not, the number of persons who subsist on daily wages, exceed the regular demand for their services?

This question is not satisfactorily answered; there is much diversity of opinion, as will appear from the following extracts. It is generally agreed that the poor are professedly willing to work.

"They will all say they are willing to work, but the fact is not so, and the number of persons, who subsist on daily wages does not in my opinion exceed the demand; for it is notorious, that when work is wanted to be done there is usually great difficulty in getting hands to perform it."

"The number is not greater than the demand in summer, but in winter all cannot find employment."

"Three-fourths; and employment in the summer season could be found for the remainder if they were disposed to seek it."

---

[5] *Southwark:* a working-class neighborhood.

"Two thirds are willing to work and those disposed and able can generally meet with some employment; the improvident always exceed the regular demand for their services."

"Many of the poor are willing to labour if they could procure employment, and we believe that the number of those who depend for subsistence on daily wages, in the city, exceeds the demand for their services."

"There no doubt are many of the labouring poor, who refuse work proffered to them at busy seasons, demanding exorbitant prices for small jobs; during the times of business it is difficult to obtain people of this description to do necessary work, but in the winter there is considerably more than can obtain employment."

Nearly allied to the preceding question is the following proposed by the board of guardians.

"What number of your paupers claim relief on the plea of want of work? Are they generally men or woman?"

It is answered generally, a great proportion, and principally women.

Query 14. Would the indigent be willing to emigrate with their families into the interior of the country in pursuit of work, provided they were assisted in such removal?

It is the almost universal opinion, that they could not be induced, except in some particular cases; "never while they are so bountifully provided for in the city; in our opinion the charitable institutions induce the poor to come here from all quarters."

Query 15. Could the poor be induced to deposit their surplus earnings in the saving banks?

It is supposed that but few have any surplus earnings, some of these it is believed might be persuaded to deposit them, if made acquainted with the advantages of such institutions, of which at present they are mostly ignorant.

"It is believed by this committee, if employers would exert themselves to impress on the minds of journeymen mechanics, the advantage which would result from depositing their surplus earnings in saving banks, much good would arise from it: a practical demonstration of the accumulation of small sums deposited in that manner, would no doubt encourage many to deposit in the saving banks during the summer months."

Query 16. Are, or are not, indigent parents unwilling to bind their children to tradesmen and for service in families? and what mode of employment do they prefer for their children?

"The poor are mostly unwilling to bind their children to services in families; they prefer placing them in situations, where they can themselves reap some emolument from their labour. We are of opinion that poor parents would not feel such reluctance in binding out their children, were masters and mistresses to adopt the kind conduct recommended by a humane author of 'treating their servants as unfortunate friends,' but how painfully reversed is their conduct in many instances." "They appear willing to bind their children to tradesmen when they arrive at the age of 10 or 12 years, and this mode they prefer to sending them to [domestic] service, as in the former case they obtain education and a trade; in the latter they cannot expect these."

"Indigent parents are unwilling to bind their children at all, but we believe a preference would be given to trades over family service. Many parents are prevented by pride from consenting to put out their children, and in many instances the larger ones are necessary in assisting the mother; others endeavour to keep children at home until they are old enough to be hired, and thus by their wages add to the general stock for the support of the whole...."

"It is customary with the poor to hire their children out at a small sum per week; a practice frequently attended with bad consequences as relates to the habits and future conduct of their offspring; many send them begging or collecting fuel."

Query 17. Sect. 1. What would be the best mode of improving the condition of the poor?

Upon this question we shall multiply extracts from the documents, as we conceive it to be of importance to exhibit the different ideas upon this interesting subject, in the language of the respective writers.

[The following is a selection of eight of the twenty-one responses included in the original report.]

"On the best mode of improving the condition of the poor some difficulties occur. Upon a review of the subject, however, two great objects present themselves, which if accomplished, may gradually reduce all the rest to insignificance. These are the removing from the labouring class all access to spirituous liquors, and furnishing them with the means of support by their industry. Whether a society embracing both objects could be formed and properly conducted, is a matter deserving of consideration. At any rate we are of opinion, that at least one for the attainment of the first should be instituted, to be composed of men of respectability and influence; and indeed of the citizens generally; who are convinced of the necessity of a reform in this particular, who should pledge themselves to discountenance the use of liquor, in persons whom they employ, to punish any breaches of the laws and to obtain the passage of such laws, as from the information which the society will be continually acquiring may be deemed expedient; and in order more fully to carry their purposes into effect, a society should be established in each ward auxiliary to the general society, which by means of committees for the districts into which the wards should be divided, should be charged with the execution of the plans of the general society. Thus a blow would be struck at the root of, (as we conceive) the greatest evil; an immense mass of information would be collected, from which the society would more effectually be able to devise and execute new plans, and extend its views towards further improving the condition of the poor. . . . "

. . .

"The propensity to vice and immorality is greatly facilitated by the great number of dram-shops and tippling-houses, where acquaintances and connexions are formed, and the habits of drunkenness and indolence take root. . . . Habitual drunkards ought to be deprived of their civil rights and have guardians appointed over them to manage their affairs, compel those to work that have no other means, and out of their earnings support themselves and families if they have any; this disfranchisement to continue until they are thoroughly reformed. A plan for this purpose it is believed may be formed, aided by law, and will easily be executed when the people at large are convinced, that by giving up licentious liberty, they will enjoy that which is rational."

. . .

"Break up tippling houses; provide sufficient schools for all the children of the poor, and obtain a law which shall oblige them to have their children educated; encourage their attendance at a place of worship on the first day of the week, and adopt such regulations in connexion with the subject, as may prevent impositions being practiced on our citizens by straggling poor from other places, who make this a resort in the winter season. . . . "

. . .

"From the observation of this committee, they are of opinion that four fifths of the poor, who now depend upon charity, principally, might be enabled to support themselves entirely.

The committee are further of opinion, that the multiplication of charitable institutions, is not attended with these benefits which a slight view of the subject, would seem to promise. These institutions have rather a tendency to produce an entire reliance upon them for support, or at least to induce the poor to believe that there is no great necessity of their individual exertions, for their own maintenance. They therefore suggest the advantage of concentrating the present charities, which would afford one great means of carrying into effect any new plan, that may be devised; at all events, there would be a greater certainty of applying the funds of these societies to proper objects, and with more advantage; for it often happens that several benevolent societies, are extending their bounty to an individual, each under the impression that no relief to the case is given but through their hands; and the poor find it to their own views of advantage, to keep their almoners as free from a knowledge of the true state of their case, as possible. . . . "

. . .

"The best mode for improving the condition of the poor would (in my opinion) be, to establish a house of employ for them, where they would be enabled to work for their subsistence, at periods when the inclemency of the season prevented them from getting employ elsewhere, which would cause a great saving to the public, and give them an opportunity to discriminate betwixt the industrious and deserving, and the indolent and worthless; the latter class of whom generally reap the greatest share, from the present mode of relieving them by distribution."[6]

. . .

"The best mode of improving the condition of the poor who generally come into the Alms-house, would be to have a penitentiary attached to the institution, in order to compel those to work who are able."

. . .

"I think it would be sound policy in the guardians of the poor to purchase a lot or square near the built parts of the city, and thereon to build small two or three story brick houses for the use of paupers, to be rented at a moderate rate, and to refuse any aid to those who did not live in these houses subject to certain rules and regulations. The objects

[6]*distribution:* outdoor relief.

of public charity thus collected in one place, could be better managed, their wants better and more cheaply supplied, and their vices more easily discerned and corrected, than when they are scattered in a thousand obscure alleys, obliged to pay an exorbitant rent for a miserable room, and which rent the corporation[7] in fact pay when the paupers are pensioners.[8] . . . "

. . .

"As a considerable portion of the poor is black, we think some measures should be taken, to prevent an increase of their number, by continual additions of those who arrive here for the purpose of being emancipated. We do not wish to be considered as being favourable to their slavery—but we believe some advantageous alterations might be made in the abolition system."

Query 17. Sect. 2d. What are the effects of soup houses established in Philadelphia?

"In such seasons as the one we have recently passed through, when to the rigours of the year, have been added a great dearth of employment and an unusually high price for provisions we do not hesitate to pronounce the soup societies a blessing to the community. We know that the sufferings which the children of the poor must necessarily experience, have by this means been greatly alleviated." . . .

Query 18. How many children can an industrious husband and wife support by daily labour?

The reports differ very widely upon this subject; some believing that only three can be supported; others 6, and others even 12 or more; according to the occupation, prudence, economy, health, and industry of the parents.

[Several tables omitted.]

. . .

Upon a review of the whole, intemperance, and the want of employment, appear to be the origin of the misery which has been so frequently witnessed; and any measures, which will either directly, or indirectly, tend to remove these causes, would be adopted by the society

---

[7] *the corporation:* the city.
[8] *pensioners:* recipients of cash outdoor relief from the city.

with the best prospect of success, towards relieving the public from a heavy burden, and rendering a class of citizens, now worse than useless, profitable to themselves, their families, and society at large—all of which is respectfully submitted.

2

The New York Society for the Prevention of Pauperism
1818

New York's Society for the Prevention of Pauperism (SPP) *led the charge to define poverty as a moral flaw, one best repaired by using community policing and the power of the state to regulate the lives of the poor. Modeled on a similar group in England, the* SPP *held the existing poor relief system responsible for the growth in urban poverty. As their founding document warned, "Indigence and helplessness will multiply nearly in the ratio of those measures which are ostensibly taken to prevent them." The author of this 1818 report was John Griscom (1774– 1852), a Columbia College chemistry professor who would become a founder of the New York House of Refuge (see Document 10) in the 1820s.*

. . . We were not insensible of the serious and alarming evils that have resulted, in various places, from misguided benevolence, and imprudent systems of relief. We knew that in Europe and America, where the greatest efforts have been made to provide for the sufferings of the poor, by high and even enormous taxation, those sufferings were increasing in a ratio much greater than the population, and were evidently augmented by the very means taken to subdue them.

We were fully prepared to believe, that without a radical change in the principles upon which public alms have been usually distributed, helplessness and poverty would continue to multiply—demands for

Report of a Committee on the Subject of Pauperism (New York: Samuel Wood and Sons, 1818).

Figure 2. *Five Points, 1827.*

Members of New York's Society for the Prevention of Pauperism decried the chaos of working-class neighborhoods like Five Points. This street scene catalogued virtually every anxiety of middle-class reformers: racial mixing, unchaperoned women, truancy, alcoholism, prostitution, poor sanitation, gambling, theatrical performances, and disorderly public behavior. McSpedon & Baker, *Five Points, 1827.* The Library Company of Philadelphia.

relief would become more and more importunate, the numerical difference between those who are able to bestow charity and those who sue for it, would gradually diminish, until the present system must fall under its own irresistible pressure, prostrating perhaps, in its ruin, some of the pillars of social order.

It might be long indeed, before such a catastrophe would be extensively felt in this free and happy country. Yet, it is really to be feared, as we apprehend, that it would not be long before some of the proximate evils of such a state of things would be perceived in our public cities, and in none, perhaps, sooner than in New-York. . . .

The indirect causes of poverty are as numerous as the frailties and vices of men. They vary with constitution, with character, and with national and local habits. Some of them lie so deeply entrenched in the weakness and depravity of human nature, as to be altogether unassailable by mere political regulation. They can be reached in no other way, than by awakening the dormant and secret energies of moral feeling.

But with a view to bring the subject committed to our charge, more definitely before the society, we have thought it right, distinctly to enumerate the more prominent of those causes of poverty, which prevail within this city. . . .

1st. IGNORANCE, arising either from inherent dullness, or from want of opportunities for improvement. This operates as a restraint upon the physical powers, preventing that exercise and cultivation of the bodily faculties by which skill is obtained, and the means of support increased. The influence of this cause, it is believed, is particularly great among the foreign poor that annually accumulate in this city.

2nd. IDLENESS. A tendency to this evil may be more or less inherent. It is greatly increased by other causes, and when it becomes habitual, it is the occasion of much suffering in families, and augments to a great amount the burden of the industrious portions of society.

3d. INTEMPERANCE IN DRINKING. This most prolific source of mischief and misery, drags in its train almost every species of suffering which afflicts the poor. This evil, in relation to poverty and vice, may be emphatically styled, the *Cause of Causes*. The box of Pandora is realized in each of the kegs of ardent spirits that stand upon the counters of the 1600 licensed grocers of this city. At a moderate computation, the money spent in the purchase of spirituous liquors would be more than sufficient to keep the whole city constantly supplied with bread. Viewing the enormous devastations of this evil upon the minds and morals of the people, we cannot but regard it as the crying and increasing sin of the nation, and as loudly demanding the solemn deliberation of our legislative assemblies.

4th. WANT OF ECONOMY. Prodigality is comparative. Among the poor, it prevails to a great extent, in an inattention to those small, but frequent savings when labour is plentiful, which may go to meet the privations of unfavourable seasons.

5th. IMPRUDENT AND HASTY MARRIAGES. This, it is believed is a fertile source of trial and poverty.

6th. LOTTERIES. The depraving nature and tendency of these allurements to hazard money, is generally admitted by those who have been most attentive to their effects. The time spent in inquiries relative to lotteries, in frequent attendance on lottery offices, the feverish anxiety which prevails relative to the success of tickets, the associations to which it leads, all contribute to divert the labourer from his employment, to weaken the tone of his morals, to consume his earnings, and consequently to increase his poverty. . . .

7th. PAWNBROKERS. The establishment of these offices is considered as very unfavourable to the independence and welfare of the middling and inferior classes. The artifices which are often practised to deceive the expectations of those who are induced, through actual distress, or by positive allurement, to trust their goods at these places, not to mention the facilities which they afford to the commission of theft, and the encouragement they give to a dependence on stratagem and cunning, rather than on the profits of honest industry, fairly entitle them, in the opinion of the committee, to a place among the *causes of Poverty.*

8th. HOUSES OF ILL FAME. The direful effects of those sinks of iniquity, upon the habits and morals of a numerous class of young men, especially of sailors and apprentices, are visible throughout the city. Open abandonment of character, vulgarity, profanity, &c. are among the inevitable consequences, as it respects our own sex, of those places of infamous resort. Their effects upon the several thousands of females within this city, who are ingulphed in those abodes of all that is vile, and all that is shocking to virtuous thought, upon the miserable victims, many of them of decent families, who are here subjected to the most cruel tyranny of their inhuman masters—upon the females, who, hardened in crime, are nightly sent from those dens of corruption to roam through the city, "seeking whom they may devour," we have not the inclination, nor is it our duty to describe. Among "the causes of poverty," those houses, where all the base-born passions are engendered—where the vilest profligacy receives a forced culture, must hold an eminent rank.

9th. THE NUMEROUS CHARITABLE INSTITUTIONS OF THE CITY. The committee by no means intend to cast an indiscriminate censure upon these institutions, nor to implicate the motives, nor even to deny the usefulness, in a certain degree, of any one of them. They have unquestionably had their foundation in motives of true Philanthropy; they have contributed to cultivate the feelings of christian charity, and to keep alive its salutary influence upon the minds of our fellow-citizens; and they have doubtless relieved thousands from the pressure of the most pinching want, from cold, from hunger, and probably in many cases, from untimely death.

But, in relation to these societies, a question of no ordinary moment presents itself to the considerate and real philanthropist. Is not the partial and temporary good which they accomplish, how acute soever the miseries they relieve, and whatever the number they may rescue from sufferings or death, more than counterbalanced, by the evils that flow from the expectations they necessarily excite; by the relaxation of industry, which such a display of benevolence tends to produce; by that reliance upon charitable aid, in case of unfavourable times, which must unavoidably tend to diminish, in the minds of the labouring classes, that wholesome anxiety to provide for the wants of a distant day, which alone can save them from a state of absolute dependance, and from becoming a burden to the community? . . .

LASTLY. Your committee would mention WAR during its prevalence, as one of the most abundant sources of poverty and vice, which the list of human corruptions comprehends. But as this evil lies out of the immediate reach of local regulation, and as we are now happily blest with a peace which we hope will be durable, it is deemed unnecessary further to notice it.

Such are the causes which are considered as the more prominent and operative in producing that amount of indigence and suffering, which awakens the charity of this city, and which has occasioned the erection of buildings for eleemosynary[1] purposes, at an expense of half a million of dollars, and which calls for the annual distribution of 90,000 dollars more. But, if the payment of this sum were the only inconvenience to be endured—trifling, indeed, in comparison would be the evils which claim our attention. Of the mass of affliction and wretchedness actually sustained, how small a portion is thus relieved! Of the quantity of misery and vice which the causes we have enumerated, with others we have not named, bring upon the city, how trifling

---

[1] *eleemosynary:* charitable.

the portion actually removed, by public or by private benevolence! Nor do we conceive it possible to remove this load of distress, by all the alms doings of which the city is capable, while the causes remain in full and active operation.

Effectually to relieve the poor, is therefore a task far more comprehensive in its nature, than simply to clothe the naked and to feed the hungry. It is, to erect barriers against the encroachments of moral degeneracy;—It is to heal the diseases of the mind;—It is, to furnish that aliment to the intellectual system which will tend to preserve it in healthful operation. . . .

We therefore proceed to point out the means, which we consider best calculated to meliorate the condition of the poorer classes, and to strike at the root of those evils which go to the increase of poverty and its attendant miseries.

We hold it to be a plain fundamental truth, that one of the most powerful incitements to an honest and honourable course of conduct, is a regard to reputation: or a desire of securing the approbation of our friends and associates. To encourage this sentiment among the poor, to inspire them with the feelings of self respect, and a regard to character, will be to introduce the very elements of reform. . . .

1st. To divide the city into very small districts, and to appoint from the members of the society, two or three visiters for each district, whose duty it shall be, to become acquainted with the inhabitants of the district, to visit frequently the families of those who are in indigent circumstances, to advise them with respect to their business, the education of their children, the economy of their houses, to administer encouragement or admonition, as they may find occasion; and in general, by preserving an open, candid, and friendly intercourse with them, to gain their confidence, and by suitable and well timed counsel, to excite them to such a course of conduct as will best promote their physical and moral welfare. The visiters to keep an accurate register of the names of all those who reside within their respective districts, to notice every change of residence, whether of single or married persons, and to annex such observations to the names of those who claim their particular attention as will enable them to give every needful information with respect to their character, reputation, habits, &c.

It may fairly be presumed, that if this scheme of inspection can be carried into full effect; if visiters can be found, who will undertake the charge, from the pure motive of philanthropy, and if, on the principles of active concert, a reference be always had to the books of the visiters, before charitable relief is extended to any individual, by any of the institutions already established, and due notice taken of the information they afford, a change will soon be perceived in the aspect of the poor. Finding that they have real friends, that their conduct is an object of solicitude, that their characters will be the subject of remark, a sense of decency, and a spirit of independence will be gradually awakened, the effects of which, must eventually be perceived in the diminution of the poor rates of the city.

2nd. To encourage and assist the labouring classes to make the most of their earnings, by promoting the establishment of a Savings Bank, or of Benefit Societies, Life Insurances, &c. The good effects of such associations have been abundantly proved in Europe and in America. Boston, Philadelphia, and Baltimore have each a Savings Bank.

3rd. To prevent, by all legal means, the access of paupers who are not entitled to a residence in the city. The plan of inspection before described will furnish the means of entirely preventing those disgraceful encroachments upon the charity of the city, which it is believed have been practised to no inconsiderable extent.

4th. To unite with the corporate authorities in the entire inhibition of street begging. There can be no reasonable excuse whatever, for this practice, more especially if the course of inspection, now recommended, be kept in operation.

5th. To aid, if it shall be deemed expedient, in furnishing employment to those who cannot procure it, either by the establishment of houses of industry, or by supplying materials for domestic labour. . . .

6th. To advise and promote the opening of places of worship in the outer wards of the city, especially in situations where licentiousness is the most prevalent. This subject is considered as one of vital importance. If, as we believe, nine tenths of the poverty and wretchedness which the city exhibits, proceeds directly or indirectly from the want of correct moral principle, and if religion is the basis of morality, then will it be admitted, that to extend the benefits of religious instruction, will be to strike at the root of that corrupt tree which sheds dreariness and penury from all its branches. That there is a lamentable deficiency of religious observance, is extremely obvious. It is questionable whether one man or woman in fifty, of the indigent, enters a place of worship three times in a year. The means are not provided for them, and they are unable to provide them for themselves. Now it has been remarked, that in the immediate vicinity of a church, it is rare to find a house devoted to lewdness or depravity. One half of the sum *annually* expended in the maintenance of the poor, would be sufficient to build three houses for public worship.

Further, if wretchedness proceed from vice, and vice, among the poor, be generally the offspring of moral and intellectual darkness, is it not a most reasonable, social duty, which the enlightened portions of society owe to the ignorant, to instruct before they condemn, to teach before they punish? . . .

7th. To promote the advancement of First day, or Sunday School Instruction, both of children and adults. We cannot but regard this kind of instruction as one of the most powerful engines of social reform, that the wisdom and benevolence of men have ever brought into operation.

8th. To contrive a plan, if possible, by which all the spontaneous charities of the town may flow into one channel, and be distributed in conformity to a well regulated system, by which deception may be prevented, and other indirect evils arising from numerous independent associations, be fairly obviated.

It appears highly probable, that if the administration of the charities of the city were so conducted, as to obviate all danger of misapplication and deception; those charities would flow with greater freedom, and that funds might occasionally be obtained, which would afford the means of erecting houses for worship, opening schools, and employing teachers, and thus direct, with greater efficacy, those materials which alone can ensure to the great fabric of society, its fairest proportions, and its longest duration.

9th. To obtain the abolition of the greater number of shops, in which spirituous liquors are sold by license. . . .

3

HEMAN HUMPHREY

On Doing Good to the Poor
1818

More than a matter of public policy, caring for the poor was a religious obligation for the majority of Americans who considered themselves Christians. Churches fed and clothed the needy in almost every locality, even as understandings of poverty varied from denomination to denomination and from congregation to congregation. The poor might constitute a blessing that allowed the devout to prove their worthiness through good deeds. The New Testament's portrayal of Jesus as a man of humble means who aided and served the desperate might inspire charitable efforts. For Heman Humphrey (1779–1861), a Congregational minister in the small town of Pittsfield, Massachusetts, the growth of poverty constituted a sign of God's anger with the moral laxity of nineteenth-century New Englanders. In this sermon delivered on a day of fasting, Humphrey outlined the causes of poverty and offered a series of curative steps for the redemption of the entire society. In his subsequent career as president of Amherst College (1823–1845) and as a leader of the temperance movement, Humphrey remained a staunch defender of religious orthodoxy and continued to express alarm at the decline of American morality.

In theorizing on the subject before us, even wise and good men have often mistaken first principles; and hence the disappointment of their fondest hopes; hence the failure of their best endeavours to mitigate the evils of pauperism. They have not taken man as he *is,* a fallen, depraved creature; naturally proud, indolent, evil and unthankful; but as he *should* be, holy, humble, industrious, conscientiously disposed to do every thing in his power to maintain himself, and thankful for the smallest favours.

It was once pretty generally supposed, and is still believed by many, that the existing ills of poverty might be cured, and the increase of it

---

Heman Humphrey, *On Doing Good to the Poor: A Sermon, Preached at Pittsfield, on the Day of the Annual Fast, April 4, 1818* (Pittsfield, Mass.: Phinehas Allen, 1818), 17–25, 40–41.

prevented, by generously and promptly feeding and clothing it. On this subject, men reason thus:—Here is a certain number of paupers and vagrant beggars, to be wholly maintained; and here are so many other poor people, to be supported, in part, out of the funds of charity. Now let us make our estimates accordingly, and then promptly follow them, with the necessary public and private appropriations. Let us generously feed and clothe the destitute, without discrimination. In this way we shall at once make up a given deficiency. We shall excite the gratitude of all whom we relieve. Our bounty will doubtless operate as a stimulus to future industry, by which many, who are now dependant, will hereafter maintain themselves; or, upon the most unfavourable calculation, should a burden equal to the present still remain, it will not, in the ordinary course of things, be augmented.

Such is the theory: but what is the testimony of facts? This seemingly benevolent plan has been tried, for a long course of years, and upon a great scale, in one of the most enlightened portions of the globe. It has also been tried, effectually, in many other places. But it has utterly disappointed the hopes and doings of charity. Many a wellfed beggar has, by proclaiming his success in the ears of the idle and unprincipled, induced ten men to embark in the same nefarious speculation. Many a charitable fund has operated as a premium upon improvidence and vice.

Many a soup-house has, to the sore disappointment of benevolence, proved a most efficient recruiting post for pauperism. The demands of poverty, in the city and in the country, have steadily increased. To meet these demands, charity has opened her hand wider, and still wider; and thus has she gone on, giving and hoping, till the poor rates in England, alone, amount to the enormous sum of *seven millions of pounds,* besides all her immense public and private charities: and till, within the space of eleven years, no less than 500,000 of her citizens were added to the list of paupers!

The same result, though not so alarming in extent, has been experienced in many parts of our own country. It is now pretty well agreed, both at home and abroad, that benevolence has been all this while employed in feeding a consumption; in throwing oil upon the fire which she would fain extinguish; and that if other means of cure cannot be found out, the case is hopeless.

Now, in this lamentable failure, there is nothing but what may be accounted for upon obvious principles.—Man, by the fall, lost the image of his Maker. He is totally depraved. Reason and conscience are dethroned and enslaved by passion and appetite. Restless as he is, labour and business are extremely irksome. Indolence and vice are his favourite elements. If he can gain a subsistence, however scanty and precarious, without the sweat of his brow, he will not work. It requires strong motives, and even pressing necessities, to rouse him to action; to make him industrious and frugal. I lay it down as a well established maxim, that no part of human industry is spontaneous. It is all the effect of habit, principle, and necessity. Take any number of human beings you please, in a state of nature, and not one of them will betake himself to any regular and laborious employment, so long as he can subsist without it. Who ever heard of an industrious savage?

If you would raise up a generation of sots, and beggars, and banditti, try the experiment in your own families. Leave them to the impulse of their inclinations. Let them do as much and as little as they please. Ply them with no motives; employ no means to make them industrious. Let them never feel the stimulus of necessity; and where, a few years hence, would be your enterprizing young men; your highly cultivated and productive fields; your trade, your domestic peace, your schools and your religion? Alas! how soon would idleness, profligacy, ignorance and barbarism demolish and sweep away all the memorials of virtue, intelligence and general prosperity. Take, then, but this single view of human nature along with you in the present investigation. Apply the remarks which have just been made, to the case in hand. First, make every allowance for the power of habit, the sense of shame and the influence of principle upon the minds of men, and how many still, if they find they can be maintained, or but half maintained, in idleness and tippling, will deliberately throw themselves and families upon your hands. Nor will the evil stop here. Make the poverty of such people honourable, or even tolerable, by your benefactions, and multitudes, who have hitherto supported themselves, will follow an example so congenial to human depravity.

Increase your charities, augment your gifts, and you add fuel to the fire. The calls of real distress will multiply faster around you, than you can possibly furnish means to relieve them. Establish a permanent charitable fund, to any amount; put half the property of the town into that fund to-morrow, and you will soon find more than enough of an intemperate, starving and ragged population, to swallow up the income.

Such, my brethren, is human nature; and in all our plans for ameliorating the condition of the poor, we must take men as they *are,* and try to make of them what they *should be.* A raging fever is not to be cured by stimulants. Poverty is not to be bribed away by costly and repeated presents. If you would cure the disease, you must have recourse to other means. You must purge out the morbid humours, and impart a new tone to the system. If you would prevent the further spread of pauperism, you must remove the causes of contagion. . . .

It is a subject of general complaint in most of our towns, that they are exceedingly infested with vagrant beggars; most of whom are excessively filthy, clamorous, impudent and unthankful; and the question is, How ought these miserable objects to be treated? My answer is, generally, with frowns and a flat denial. This may sound harsh; but it is deliberately, and I hope kindly spoken. Experience has proved, over and over, a thousand times, that most of these digusting fragments of humanity are arrant imposters. It is their trade to deceive the credulous, and to subsist upon the earnings of industry. They "will not work," and therefore, "neither should they eat." By feeding and clothing, and occasionally giving them money, you not only encourage them to continue their depredations upon society; but you inflict a lasting injury upon themselves. Where a beggar happens to have some shame and conscience still lingering about him at the commencement of his career, these uncomfortable companions will soon be wholly discarded. And when all self-respect, when all regard for character is gone, what can you look for, from a depraved creature like man? . . .

. . . Human nature is every where the same; and there is no philosophical truth more firmly established than this, that like causes produce like effects. If the system has not yet had time to develope all its haggard and diabolical features, in the United States, it is surely and steadily tending to the fullest maturity of sin and suffering.

Who does not know, that most of those loathsome, strolling wretches who infest our towns, are addicted to lying, swearing, drunkenness and theft. How many of them seem to take it for granted, that whatever you possess is theirs, and most outrageously abuse you, in your own houses, if you venture to deny them. How many of these insufferable drones and impostors have you found intoxicated, with the very money which you had given them to procure a night's lodging at the public house. How often have they profanely assailed you with quotations from scripture, and dreadful imprecations of divine vengeance, when you have thought it your duty to send them away empty. Which of you would trust one of them alone, for a moment, in a room where you have any thing valuable that can be taken away? And are such impositions and abuses as these to be tolerated? Can we justify ourselves before God, in squandering upon these impious vagabonds what ought to be given away in real charity? No; let the harpies find, that what they get costs much more than it is worth.

Figure 3.   *Intemperance and Poverty.*
Heman Humphrey considered intemperance "by far the greatest and most horrible of all causes of pauperism" in the United States. The 1810s witnessed the formation of local temperance societies and the publication of numerous tracts denouncing the excessive use of liquor. Temperance literature carefully invoked gendered notions of familial obligation to jolt drinkers into sobriety. This disgusting graphic appeared in an anti-alcohol treatise penned by Parson Weems, who was better known for mythologizing the story of young George Washington and the cherry tree.
M. L. Weems, *The Drunkard's Looking Glass* (Philadelphia, 1818), 39. The Library Company of Philadelphia.

Make their nefarious trade as disgraceful and unprofitable as possible, and you will soon be freed from their impertinence. Let the same course be pursued every where, and I hesitate not to say, that it must produce a great blessing to the vagrants themselves. It will drive most of them to labour for their own support; and thus, while their best good is promoted, the public will be relieved from a most unreasonable burden. In the mean time, the few who are really incapable of self-support, will find their way to almshouses and other asylums, where they will, in general, be made far more comfortable than they are, or can be, in their present vagrant course of life.

Upon the whole, I am constrained, brethren, to give it as my deliberate opinion, that more than *nine tenths* of all that is bestowed upon itinerant beggars, in the shape of charity, is far worse than thrown away. It goes to feed a nest of vipers. It fearfully increases the evil which it is intended to relieve.

But here, benevolence may ask, what then ought to be done? Shall all these miserable beings be spurned from every door, and left to starve in the streets? No, my brethren, far from it. Your laws have made ample provision for their support; and under some of the best regulations, I believe, that human wisdom has ever devised....

Our ancestors have not devolved upon us the difficult task of framing, in a degenerate age, all the necessary laws for the punishment of evil doers, the prevention of crimes, the encouragement of sobriety and industry; and whatever else is essential to the well-being of society. Almost every thing is prepared to our hands, and has come down to us from our ancestors, the pious fathers of New-England. I need not say, how much those illustrious founders of our happy republic have been ridiculed and vilified, as weak, and bigoted, and fanatical, by some of their puny and degenerate offspring. But I will say, without fear of contradiction, that they were higher from their shoulders and upward, than their tallest revilers; that there were men among them, who, for rectitude of principle, soundness of judgment, largeness of views, and piety of heart, would not suffer in comparison with the wisest and best legislators of any age or country. The whole world may be challenged to produce a code of laws, which, for the government of a free and enlightened people, can be compared, for one moment, with those which they bequeathed to posterity.

It is wonderful to observe, in their early statutes and institutions, with what prospective, I had almost said prophetic sagacity, they guarded against almost every danger, civil, political, moral and religious, which might menace the security and prosperity of their descendants. Had the laws which they framed been faithfully executed; had their noble spirit proved hereditary; had their "mantle" fallen upon their children, and then upon their children's children, vice would never have gained its present alarming ascendency. The evils and sufferings of poverty would have been comparatively few and light. It is by *degeneracy* that we have brought upon ourselves these heavy burdens, and that we stand exposed to still greater evils. We have stood by, with our arms folded, and permitted the enemy to make wide breaches in our walls; to drive our sentinels before them, and to overawe the whole garrison. Let us now, at length, arise, expel these "armies of the aliens;" build up these breaches; adhere steadily to the principles and measures of our forefathers, and we shall reap a rich harvest of public and private blessings.

We have only to repair the machinery which our ancestors have bequeathed us; to brush away the cobwebs and rub off the rust, which have accumulated through disuse; to put and keep the wheels and springs in motion, and the reformation, which every good man prays for, will follow almost of course. . . .

4

JOSEPH TUCKERMAN

Of Intellectually and Morally Neglected Children
c. 1828

Joseph Tuckerman (1778–1840) had more firsthand experience with the urban poor than did Heman Humphrey. After graduating from Harvard College and pursuing a ministerial career, Tuckerman became the Unitarian Church's Minister at Large to the Poor of Boston. From this post, Tuckerman visited with poor families, raised funds for their relief, and participated in public debates on welfare policies. Tuckerman understood the precarious position of laboring families and the degree to which temporary unemployment or illness might thrust a self-sufficient household on to public relief. Yet Tuckerman also stressed the relationship of criminality and alcoholism to poverty. For Tuckerman, Christian benevolence, moral policing, and public education provided the best methods of alleviating poverty.

Joseph Tuckerman on the Elevation of the Poor, ed. E. E. Hale (Boston: Roberts Brothers, 1874; reprint, New York: Arno Press, 1971), 119–26.

... Allow me to remark that, while I would not ascribe the licentiousness, the dishonesty, or the crime of any character in society to any single cause, — for the causes of these evils are many and sometimes very complicated, — the fact of the very peculiar connection between intemperance and abject pauperism and crime, which has been established beyond contradiction by the investigations which have been made of this subject within the last five years, demands the very serious attention not only of the statesman and the philanthropist, but of every parent and of every individual who is interested in the well-being of the community in which he lives. ... These examinations have brought to light the facts, — before, indeed, supposed, but now proved, — first, that the instance can hardly be found of a convict who at the time of his conviction was not intemperate; and, secondly, that three-fourths of the inmates of almshouses were brought to the abjectness and degradation in which they are seen there by intemperance. In view of these facts, then, I take the ground that, whatever goes to prove that intemperance is a cause, and a prevailing cause, of pauperism and crime, goes equally to prove, first, that every intemperate lad or young man, unless recovered from his intemperance, will probably fall into pauperism or crime, or into both; and, secondly, that the temptations and the facilities to an early love and use of ardent spirits are direct means, to the extent to which they operate, of producing paupers and criminals in the city, in the commonwealth, and in our country. ...

... How often have I wished that I could bring those who have a strong general interest in the well-being of society, and whose opinions exert a most important influence where I have no power, into the families of poor and intemperate parents. There let them see in what wretched rooms these unhappy beings are sometimes lodged; rooms as cold as wide chinks and broken windows can make them; the poor, broken, and scanty furniture; and the bed not unfrequently lying upon the floor, and without a bedstead, and, it may be, consisting only of straw or of shavings. There let them see to what deep degradation our nature may be brought through abandonment to the sin in which these parents are living. Will it be said that parents in this condition are beyond the reach even of hope? I think otherwise; for no one is to be considered or treated as beyond hope while God shall spare him. But I am not now pleading for these parents. I would direct attention to *their children*. Here are boys and girls with bodies which are seldom washed, and which are covered at best with filthy and tattered garments. These children probably go to no school; and they learn nothing but from the example of those with whom they associate. They are unaccustomed to any regularity in their meals, and they look for their food perhaps almost as much from home as at home. They are now, it may be, caressed with the extravagance of intoxicated affection, and now beaten with the extravagance of intoxicated anger. They are every day deceived by their parents, and they every day in turn deceive them. At one hour they are kept at work to procure fuel, or perform some other service; and in the next, are allowed to go where they will, and to do what they will. They hear profaneness every day, and see intemperance, and witness parental contests; and are daily the companions of those who live amidst the same scenes, and are forming under the same influences. They are allowed, also, not only to drain the cup which an intemperate father or mother has not quite emptied, but their portion of it is sometimes given to them. If they are advised or encouraged by these guardians of their morals, it is to be more wary, more cunning, more artful. Not unfrequently, also, do these children fall into the service of the lowest of the profligate. They are ready for any guilty service within their power, by which they may earn any thing; and they have not an association with wrong, but the fear of detection and of punishment. What, then, is to be expected from these children? Is it surprising that very early they become greatly depraved? I have spoken, indeed, of the most degraded parents and of the most exposed children. But there are more of these parents and children, even in our greatly favored city, than would be suspected by those who know those among whom they live only as they pass them in the street. And there are children of other poor parents, especially of poor widows, who, though they have in this respect no evil example at home, are yet under but a feeble parental restraint, and are associates and learners of the language, and sharers of the occupations and the pleasures, of those whose very homes are schools of the grossest depravity. I pray, then, that it may be known and thought worthy of remembrance, that we have children of this class in our city, who, if neglected as they now are, as certainly as they live will become paupers and criminals. And on whom will fall the heaviest responsibility for their guilt and misery, but on those to whom God has given all the means of saving them, and who fail to use these means for the purposes for which he gave them? . . .

Is it asked, what are the remedies of these evils, and what the means for their prevention? I answer, that they are not far off; nor, if we were truly disposed to avail ourselves of them, difficult to be obtained. But little thought or care is yet given to these subjects compared with the greatness of the interests which are comprehended in them. Public sentiment is yet vague respecting the causes of pauperism and crime; and new and more efficient measures should be taken to bring these subjects, in all their relations and bearings, before the whole body of our citizens. I would say, therefore, in the first place, that if a few of our most intelligent and philanthropic men, men of leisure and influence, would unite for the study of these subjects; not merely or principally by consulting books, but by an extensive personal communication with the poor and with criminals; if these gentlemen would meet frequently—for example, one evening in every week—to bring together their facts and to compare their opinions; if they would occasionally publish these facts and opinions with the sanction of their names; and, when they shall see clearly what are the demands of justice, of humanity, and of religion, if they would combine their efforts, now for the suppression of one and now of another of the springs of evil, and now to obtain one and now another establishment for the salvation and greatest happiness of those who must otherwise be irretrievably lost to all the higher purposes of their being, a great and glorious reform might soon be effected in our city. Am I told that the plan of such an association is impracticable? I ask, why? And I appeal to the sober judgment of the intelligent, the affluent, and influential. Is a greater service here demanded than is due from those whom God has greatly blessed to the poor and degraded and miserable around us? Is it more than God will require from those to whom he has given the means of saving and blessing hundreds, and perhaps thousands, of their race? There is no service on earth from which a higher good will result to those who engage in it. A few judicious and energetic minds, combined and resolved to accomplish all which they may for the suppression of pauperism and crime, would accumulate for themselves, in this work, a better treasure than all their wealth, let them be as rich as they may; and, in a few years, might do more for the advancement of society than, without these services, would probably be accomplished in half a century. . . .

Private Benevolence
and Moral Cures for Poverty

5

The Friendly Society of St. Thomas's African Church
1797

Organized around a common ethnicity, religion, or trade, mutual aid societies had long served as a form of life insurance for members of a given community. Twenty-seven Scotsmen living in Boston founded the first mutual aid society in colonial America in 1657. Members of such associations paid annual dues that guaranteed them relief in the case of a financial emergency brought about by illness, accident, or unemployment. When a member died, mutual aid societies paid for a respectable burial and provided payments to widows and orphaned children. When free African American residents of Philadelphia began to develop community organizations in the decades after the American Revolution, black mutual aid societies followed on the heels of independent black churches. Absalom Jones, who had been enslaved until nearly forty years old, led the effort to found St. Thomas's African Church in 1794. The congregation was formally affiliated with the Episcopalian church but maintained its autonomy as an African American institution. Its Friendly Society was one of fourteen black mutual aid societies operating in Philadelphia before 1812. Such voluntary associations were essential to the economic and communal self-reliance of free blacks at a time when their status in larger American society remained unclear.

The Constitution of the Friendly Society of St. Thomas's African Church of Philadelphia (Philadelphia: W. W. Woodward, 1797).

67

CONSTITUTION, &c.

WHEREAS we the Subscribers, members of the African Episcopal Church, called ST. THOMAS'S, in the City of Philadelphia, frequently conversing on that most amiable of all the social virtues, Charity, and feeling a desire to promote it in the most consistent manner, as far as our circumstances in life will admit, at the same time to make our undertaking as permanently useful as possible, have, and hereby do, conclude to associate and unite ourselves together, by the name, title and description of "THE FRIENDLY SOCIETY OF ST. THOMAS'S AFRICAN CHURCH, OF PHILADELPHIA," under the following

Regulations:

I. THE Officers of the Society shall consist of a President, Vice-President, Treasurer, Secretary, and a Committee of Seven Members. . . .

II. WE bind ourselves, and do hereby agree, to meet monthly in a convenient place, to be procured by the committee. At all and every such meeting each and every member, and such as may hereafter become members of this Society, shall deposit one quarter of a dollar into the hands of the President, who shall cause the Secretary to credit each member for every such payment, in a book to be kept fair and correct for that purpose, bearing the date of the payment. . . .

III. THE duty of the President shall be as is expressed in the II. Article, together with that of keeping order and decorum in the Society during the meeting thereof. The duty of the Committee shall be to call delinquent members to account, and make report thereof to the Society: During the recess thereof the Committee shall visit such members of the Society as reside within their district, and if a majority of them be of the judgment that the member so visited stands in need of assistance, they shall (with the consent of the President) have power to draw on the Treasurer for such sums of money as they conjointly may think requisite, not exceeding one and a half dollar per week to each member, during his inability. . . .

IV. THE payments made by the members to the Society, shall be disposed of only for the relief and support of the orphans and widows of deceased members (so long as the widows shall remain unmarried) and for the relief of necessitous members; after which, if the funds of the Society will afford it, to any other charitable purpose that the President and a majority of the committee may deem necessary. . . .

VII. As the business of the Committee may become arduous, such as visiting the sick, inspecting their circumstances, and supplying their necessities, with other duties already pointed out, it is agreed that they shall continue in office only twelve months, unless again elected. . . .

IX. IF any member neglect meeting at the slated monthly meeting, he shall for every such neglect forfeit and pay One Eighth of a Dollar.

X. IN case of the death of any member of the society, without leaving sufficient property for his interment, the Committee shall cause him to be buried in a plain and decent manner from the Society's fund. . . .

6

The Providence Female Society for the Relief of Indigent Women and Children

1801

Starting in the 1790s, women's benevolent organizations appeared in many cities. With names like the Aimwell Society or the Impartial Humane Society, women-led charities orchestrated relief measures that other private organizations and public officials would imitate in the coming decades: screening aid recipients through home visitation, bringing children out of poor households and placing them in institutions, and making relief payments dependent upon labor. Women's charities often distributed cloth, which poor women could use to make clothing for their families or to sell back to the managers in exchange for food and firewood. In their fund-raising appeals, women's charities relied heavily on the rhetoric of female dependence and invariably invoked the image of a helpless widow. Yet the organizational activities of benevolent women suggest that middle- and upper-class females were finding new routes to independence in the early republic.

The Constitution of the Providence Female Society for the Relief of Indigent Women and Children (Providence: John Carter Jr., 1801).

THE Ladies of Providence, deeply impressed with the pitiable situation of the indigent part of their sex, and sensible the efforts of individuals must be circumscribed within very narrow limits, have, they trust, under the auspices of Divine Providence, formed themselves into a "Society for the relief of indigent Women and Children."

The Author of nature, or custom, has devolved on them the important duty of implanting first principles into the expanding mind of Childhood, and on them much of their future usefulness and happiness depends. To give an opportunity to the disconsolate Widow to feel the honest pride of giving bread to her offspring by her own industry; to direct the first steps of childhood in the paths of virtue, to smooth the bed of sickness, and to stretch forth the hand of charity to sustain the tottering steps of age, fainting under a lengthened pilgrimage, will to the feeling mind procure an unceasing source of heart-felt satisfaction; and when their Lord shall come, they may with humility say, "Lord, I have added another to the talent thou hast given me." Who would not relinquish a frivolous amusement, or a useless ornament, to enjoy that most estimable of all pleasures, an approving conscience?

As a tribute justly due to the Young Ladies, it should be mentioned, that they have come forward with alacrity and zeal to support this institution. And it is hoped by a prudent management of their own little concerns, and by proper observations and reflections, they will in time be qualified to discharge the duties of office with honour to themselves and advantage to society. . . .

Members

Shall be admitted into the Society by a vote of the Board of Directors. Besides such donations as her charity may suggest, every Member shall annually subscribe the sum of Three Dollars, to be paid at the anniversary meeting.

The Direction

Of the affairs of the Society shall be vested in a first and second Directress, a Secretary, a Treasurer, and four Managers for the summers, and six for the winter season. . . .

The portion of the Society's bounty to be expended every month, shall be divided among the Managers only, and their several shares applied by each, at discretion, to the proper objects. Any member of the Society may make known to the Managers such objects of charity as fall within her knowledge.

Every manager shall insert in a book kept for that purpose the names, places of abode and circumstances, of the persons whom she relieves; together with the names and ages of their children, and the amount and kind of relief granted each family, which book shall be presented at every meeting of the Managers, and punctually sent by those who cannot attend.

Every Manager shall endeavour to find schools for the children on her book, and places in sober virtuous families for such of them as may be fit for service. . . .

The Managers shall exert themselves to create and maintain habits of industry among their applicants, by furnishing them as far as possible with suitable employment. At the end of every month the Managers shall make up their accounts, and give a receipt to the Treasurer for the amount of their expenditures.

Relief shall not be granted to any applicants until they have been visited at their dwelling by one of the Managers, and particular enquiry be made into their characters and circumstances. Immorality excludes from the patronage of the Society.

No applicant, unless in special cases, of which the Board shall judge, shall be relieved, who refused to put to service or trade such of her children as are fit, and to place the younger ones, of a proper age, at schools. Relief shall be given in necessaries;[1] never in money, but by a vote of the Board.

As soon as the funds of the Society are sufficiently large, a suitable house shall be provided, and a Governess engaged to superintend a small number (at first) of female children from five to ten years of age, where they shall be taught to read, write, sew, and perform every branch of domestic business—they shall be clothed alike in plain attire, and encouraged in good behavior by suitable tokens of approbation from the board at their quarterly meetings. Any one to whom a child is indentured, who is upwards of ten years of age, and has been taught to read, write and sew, shall pay the Society ten dollars, which shall be given her at the expiration of her service, if her conduct shall have merited the approbation of the Board. The Children shall be taught reading and writing an hour twice each day; after which they

---

[1] *necessaries:* supplies like fuel, flour, and cloth.

shall return to their domestic avocations. The Governess shall lead
the Children every Sabbath to Public Worship.

The Funds

Of the Society which arise from annual subscriptions, and donations
from Ladies and Gentlemen, shall in part be expended in the purchase
of a stock of fuel, other necessaries, and of materials for the employment of Women: and such a part as the Society may judge advisable
shall be appropriated by the Ladies in office to the establishment of a
permanent fund.

The Society of Females, for the Relief of Indigent Women and Children, was proposed in March, and organized on the first Wednesday
of April, 1800. Twenty-three poor women have been employed, and
five sick persons have been supplied with money to procure medicine
and wood. . . .

At the semi-annual meeting the Managers received two hundred
and twenty-five dollars; they purchased one piece of coating, one of
kersey, one of ravens duck, three of baizes, and six of checks.[2] Thirty-
six outside jackets with baize linings, five under jackets, and twenty
pair of trowsers, have been made of the thick cloth, and twelve pair of
trowsers of the duck; thirty-seven baize and thirty-eight check shirts,
all of which have been sold, except some articles of thick cloathing.
The Managers have just purchased two hundred yards of checks, and
if they had twice that quantity it would not supply their applicants constantly with work. Many painful sensations have been excited in the
breasts of the Managers, by being under the necessity of refusing several who have urgently and repeatedly requested work. It is however
presumed their abilities will not be so circumscribed another year, as
the amount of sales will be added to the annual subscription.

[2]These are different types of fabric.

7

The Female Humane Association
Charity School

1803

*Presuming that poverty and its attendant vices were passed from genera-
tion to generation, charity organizations devoted much attention to the
children of poor parents. Some groups relieved widowed women by
schooling their children and apprenticing them into more prosperous
families. Although states maintained control over the legal apparatus of
indenture, groups like Baltimore's Female Humane Association (FHA)
funneled poor children into families that needed extra labor and were
able to feed an additional mouth. The FHA's charity school accepted girls
between the ages of seven and fourteen, with the expectation that they
would receive three years of education before being bound out to live in
families as domestic servants. Young "scholars" learned reading, writing,
arithmetic, and sewing. In this 1803 report to its donors, the FHA provided a testimonial from a group of satisfied employers: "The said children are orderly, quiet, and industrious, and promise, according to their
conditions in life, to be useful members of society."*

Some time in the fall of the year 1798, several Ladies of Baltimore, taking in their consideration the poverty, and consequent sufferings of
indigent women, during the inclement season of winter, Resolved to
form a systematic plan for affording them relief. They accordingly
established a Society called THE FEMALE HUMANE ASSOCIATION, held
regular meetings for the transaction of business, and collected from
the generous citizens considerable sums of money. During the winter of 1798–1799, the monies so collected were faithfully distributed
among all who became the objects of their peculiar care, according to
their several necessities. In the execution of this charity, which the
Ladies did actually perform in person, they had daily before their eyes
not only the scenes of complicated misery themselves, but the causes
which had originally led thereto, that is, the abandoned state of the

*A Brief Account of the Female Humane Association Charity School, of the City of Balti-
more* (Baltimore: Warner and Hanna, 1803).

rising generation, particularly the female part thereof, many of whom were literally raised in the streets in filthiness, rags, and vice. To remedy the evil in its source, to snatch the child from a fate similar to that of its mother, was considered by the Ladies an important public work; for the success of any scheme to ameliorate the condition of such objects, would not only lessen the demand on the public for annual contributions, but it would actually increase the number of those whose labor would be useful to the community. The subject was often mentioned among the Ladies at their meetings, and they as often concurred unanimously in the propriety of establishing a Charity School for the Education and Relief of Poor Female Children. Accordingly, a subscription was opened for the purpose, which by the 23d June, 1800, was sufficiently filled to commence the work. The school was opened under the direction of Mrs. Chapelle, and the children admitted thereinto were invariably taken from the lowest conditions in life; many, nay most of whom were, when taken into the school, not only destitute of common decency in their deportment, but wholly ignorant of the first principles of right and wrong; in truth some of them might have been called savages, whom it was necessary first to civilize, before they would be received into a reputable situation to obtain their living by domestic labor. . . .

[Since opening,] fifty Poor Female Children had been received into the School, cloathed, educated, and some of them boarded, of which number twenty-three had received their education, and been placed in reputable families for the purpose of maintaining themselves by domestic labor and employment. . . .

The Female Directors have made it a rule in all instances to board orphan children taken into the school, and such also where the morals of the children would probably be corrupted by remaining any portion of their time with their mothers; in other instances the children have received their boarding with their parents, or in respectable families, and attended school at regular and stated hours of meeting. It not unfrequently happens that families have consented to board a poor female child on the condition that it shall be bound to them when fit for service, but in all such cases the will of the parents is obtained before the child is admitted to the school. By thus procuring board for the children out of the school, the Directors have been enabled to extend the charity to a greater number of objects. . . .

8

EZRA STILES ELY

Preacher to the Poor in New York
1811

When Ezra Stiles Ely (1786–1861) first arrived at the New York Almshouse in June 1810, the young, energetic chaplain harbored hopes of redeeming a lost flock: "Rarely have I had the pleasure of witnessing, in any audience, more lively gratitude for the glorious Gospel of the grace of God." Recording two years of his labors among the institutionalized poor, Ely celebrated a deathbed conversion or a meeting with a pious widow. Of course, he also found the work exhausting and the sights and sounds overwhelming. After 270 pages of "poverty, misery, and madness," Ely allowed that his reader "may congratulate himself, that he has been a witness of solemn scenes, without experiencing the inconveniences of one, who has been personally concerned in them."

JANUARY 10, 1811

After preaching this evening to the poor in the Almshouse, I went by request to pray with two females, who have attended on my ministry, and are now confined to their beds. One is an aged widow, who is pious, and who, I believe, will recover to limp along through life, on two crutches, to ever-lasting glory. She will recover, to suffer more pain, and peddle pin-cushions to procure some of the conveniences of life, which cannot be distributed in public Almshouses. O! it is astonishing that the heirs of heaven should be found in such circumstances; that the friends of Jesus, who are to share the felicity of heaven with him, should be made meek for glory, through extreme humiliation!

JANUARY 19, 1811

Sympathy is natural and amiable; but *benevolence,* when exercised by a fallen man, is supernatural and holy. Would to God that the two were

---

Ezra Stiles Ely, *The Journal of the Stated Preacher to the Hospital and Almshouse, in the City of New-York, for the Year of Our Lord 1811* (New York: Whiting and Watson, 1812); *The Second Journal of the Stated Preacher to the Hospital and Almshouse, in the City of New-York, For a part of the year of our Lord 1813* (Philadelphia: M. Carey, 1815).

united in every human heart! Possibly both have been exercised in the relief of a certain poor widow, whose husband, a carman, died about a year since; leaving her, after she had defrayed the expenses of his sickness and burial, nothing for her support, but ten children. Four of these are able to provide for themselves, and one or two can give some assistance to the mother, by tending the four younger children, while the mother washes or sews for the necessaries of life. For eight months I have known this woman and her family. She is a professor of religion; and more, she is pious. Her children are neat and industrious. For a single room she pays twenty-five dollars, yearly rent; and earns a part of this by sewing nankeen[1] pantaloons and common shirts, for *the eighth of a dollar* for each garment. This I find to be the common price of job-work; so that the poor widows who will support themselves, must be content with *one shilling,* while the purchasers pay *many shillings* for the same work. All who sell ought to have lawful gain, but the poor, who perform the work, ought to receive at least half of that sum which is charged for making of apparel. Some of the children attend that benevolent Institution, "The New-York Free School," and if the Lord shall spare them, I doubt not will make useful mechanics. When this widow was in her most destitute condition, before she could gather something to begin the world anew, with her fatherless children, a young man of generous, native feelings, who never saw her, sent five dollars for her relief. This same man of tenderness, however, gave that for which he was indebted, and soon after defrauded many of his friends. Alas! alas! Why had not this youth *benevolence,* as well as *sympathy!* Another young man, who is poor indeed, but whom providence has hitherto protected, has more than once divided with the family, when almost destitute of wood and bread, his last dollar. The pride of doing good, or sympathy, or *something else,* may have actuated him. God searches his heart!

To give to the street beggars of this city, is not well directed charity. Those persons who have large families, who make great exertions to live out of the Almshouse, when they are almost driven into it by want, are the proper objects for pecuniary assistance.

The wind blew the piercing cold from the north; but the southern sun illuminated the abode of the widow. The children had recovered their ruddy countenances, and were seated round a frugal fire. They had a little wood still remaining and a load of bread in reserve. The widow was restored to her wonted strength, from the debility induced by long watchings with misery; and contentment was in her countenance. The

---

[1] *nankeen:* yellow cotton fabric.

sight gave new vigour to a heart which had been depressed with remembrance of wretchedness it could not dispel.

FEBRUARY 3, 1811
... Several abandoned women listened to my discourse to-day; and among them was a beautiful girl of only fifteen years of age. It was astonishing to see so fair and young a person as M.D. in such a situation. She was brought [to] the Hospital by her father, who has two other daughters beside this, who have been patients in this Institution. The eldest sister led the way; the younger sisters followed. In early childhood they were all left motherless; and the father, as is commonly the case with labouring men, had no time to stand sentinel over the chastity of three fair daughters.

FEBRUARY 10, 1811
... The deluded child of fifteen years, M.D. was present, and paid solemn attention. But she is sick now; and many are serious while a fever rages in their blood, who with returning health, return to their former stupidity. This unfortunate I design to trace, if possible in her future course. It cannot be a long one; unless God should reclaim her by the power of the Gospel. Should she evince a disposition to live a moral life in future, must she be turned out again upon the world, to encounter strong temptation? The Hospital is designed for the sick, and must not therefore be occupied by the sound. When she is restored to health, she must return to a worthless father's house, where she will find the sisters who seduced her. The eldest took her to a dancing house, provided a gallant for her, and after much solicitation, persuaded her to become a mistress. M—— thinks she should never have yielded, had it not been for the precept and example of this syren sister. The three daughters have all been ensnared by their beauty, pride, and idleness. No mother taught them to be industrious; no mother warned them of the horrible pit into which they have fallen. Their father thinks it enough to provide himself food and drink. By what profession, then could they live; by what art could they adorn their persons? Under such circumstances, where there is no fear of God, an

---

[2]M.D. reappeared in the almshouse on September 6, 1811, "covered with filth." According to Ely, she had been on the way to recovery, when a young man from the almshouse had lured her away: "His protection was of short duration; his money was soon gone; she returned to the practice of Corinth, and multiplied abominations, more than her sisters Samaria and Sodom. Extreme sickness was the result; and having lodged for a few nights in a cellar with blacks, she was brought to the Almshouse." Not sparing any judgments, Ely concluded his remarks by noting, "The way of lewdness is the shortest way to hell."

effectual repulsion of insidious approaches, a persevering struggle against temptation, need not be expected. It will never be found.[2] . . .

In such a city as this, in which are not less than seven thousand females of this description, it is devoutly to be desired, that some retreat should be afforded to those, who, from any cause, are willing to relinquish their vices; and that some association should be formed, which shall save at least a few from what they deem the necessity of prostituting themselves for a piece of bread.[3]

MARCH 13, 1811

. . . Lastly, I visited the widow and the fatherless, to learn their present situation. A few days ago I was at the abode of the same woman, and her little son was dangerously sick. She watched with him incessantly, which made me apprehensive that I should find her ill; and I was not disappointed. The little boy saw me coming, and welcomed me with a smile; but the mother was almost insensible; was confined to the bed; had sent for no physician; and had no other nurse than her half-recovered child. This woman, I positively know, has been industrious, and poverty in her case is not her fault; unless it is a crime to find needles and silk, to close and bind Morocco shoes at the rate of four shillings for twelve pair, when every cord of wood costs her more money than she can accumulate in a month.

MARCH 24, 1811

When we attempt to praise God in the Almshouse, the dialect of almost every nation is heard; for the English, Scotch, Irish, Dutch, German, French, Spanish, and Italian, as well as the American poor, have met together. What some of the foreigners want in pronunciation, they more than make up in their musical notes. I have become, now, so accustomed to this confusion of dialects that it does not disturb my devotion. Nine persons are dangerously sick in the room where I preached this morning. One of them was well last Thursday evening, attended service in the blind ward, and urged me to preach in her room to-day, with which request I complied; and possibly she may have heard her last sermon. She is now burning with a fever. She is a widow of good report, of amiable countenance, and of exemplary

[3]According to census returns for 1810, there were not more than 35,000 females between the ages of 10 and 44 in the city. By Ely's count, then, one in five was at risk of engaging in prostitution. Ely envisioned the founding of a Magdalen Society to rescue fallen women. When one finally appeared a few decades later, it became the object of public ridicule when its leader, Reverend John McDowall, estimated that there were 10,000 prostitutes in the city.

deportment. She has one little daughter of eight years of age. The poor-house has become her home, in consequence of a "white swelling" on one of her limbs, which is incurable, and utterly prevents her from labour. Poor woman! Her trials are great; but they will be sanctified to her good, and the divine glory; for she is a child of the most High, a daughter of the Lord Almighty. . . .

I turned to a Scotchman, in the same room, who on the fourth day of this month commenced his eighty-fifth year. He told me in the broad dialect of the land of his nativity, that he was "very auld, and without feeling a'most. I cannae e'en feel," said he, laying his hand on his vest, "to button my clothes."

. . . When I left him, he thanked me for a little attention to "an auld mon." While I was coming out, two other persons of seventy years arose to pay their respects to me. One was a tall, pale, hoary-headed man; and the other was blind. When I exhorted them to pray, the tears of the former fell upon his frosted beard. They said, that in such a noisy place, they found it difficult to pour out their hearts to God in any corner, but in the night, when most around them were asleep, they always attempted it.

I could easily believe their assertion, for on descending and crossing the yard, I met not less than one hundred little children, without any one to restrain them, playing all manner of gambols, and roaring like the young bears of the wilderness.

APRIL 21, 1811

The most pitiable object, whom I have seen of late, is an Irish woman, who is dangerously sick of a fever in the Almshouse. She was a good mother, and wife, before her husband deserted her; and she is a good mother still. From every one, who has known her, I learn a favourable account of her moral conduct. To-day she would have melted any heart. Four little children surrounded her bed, who were all of them like herself, and all so much like one another, that nothing but stature seemed to distinguish one from the other. All of them were crying for their poor mother. The whole family lately came from Ireland, but the husband has left her with her babes to languish, and perhaps to die, without a friend. Alas! that drunkenness should, in this country, transform a generous and wildly enthusiastic son of Erin into something worse than a brute! In Hibernia,[4] it is probable that this same fellow would have divided his last potatoe with his superannuated grandmother; or would have shed his blood in defence of his wife and children; but here, where

---

[4]*Erin, Hibernia:* Ireland.

ardent spirits are sold for six shillings by the gallon, wife children, relatives, and friends, may all go to the Almshouse, or even to "potter's field,"[5] for a glass of grog. It is said that a newly naturalized citizen, to induce some of his countrymen to immigrate to this country, wrote to his friend, "that in America a man might get drunk twice for sixpence!" This is too true!

MAY 19, 1811

... Ten persons were confined to their beds in the room in the Hospital which was this afternoon visited by the word of the Lord; and one of them, who seemed unusually tender upon religious subjects, told me in conversation, that many had been the troubles of his life, "but they are not worthy to be named; for I have deserved them all, and I think that they have been for my good." He has been born in England, bred a brewer, and for some time past, had been a journeyman at his trade in this city. On the first of May, a time when half of the poor remove from one shed to another, he was left houseless for the night.[6] The room which he occupied, had been let to another, who could pay a higher rent. He could not, on that day, procure another tenement; and the new occupant, according to the custom of this good city, cast the furniture of T—— T—— into the street. To preserve his goods during the night, the brewer seated himself on a stoop beside them. When all was silence but the hourly rap of the watchmen on the pavement, he fell asleep. A young rogue passed that way, and undertook to search the sleeper's pockets, in which he found some money; but could not make good his retreat, without arousing his plundered neighbour. The brewer gave him chase, and followed him into a cellar. This is the last that he remembers of the events of the night, but in the morning he was found alone, with a bruised head and a broken leg. "It is all well, however," said he, concluding his tale with a sigh, "for the sufferings of the present state are not worthy to be compared with the glory which shall be revealed in us."

MAY 21, 1811

The fire has greatly increased the population in my dominions.[7] This evening the doors were open into three wards in the Almshouse, so that many more than usual listened to my discourse. It was a solemn

---

[5]*potter's field:* public burial ground.

[6]In New York City, almost all leases expired on April 30, which generated an intense flurry of activity as the city's residents reshuffled themselves on May 1.

[7]Two days earlier, a huge fire had torn through Manhattan.

evening to many, and God grant that the persons burned out of home, may derive some spiritual advantage from the affliction.

AUGUST 29, 1811

. . . Mrs. M—— S——, who is bloated with the dropsy, discovered so much concern for her youngest son, that a young man went in search of him, to procure him a lodging in the Almshouse. The lad was found with a family, which resides in a cellar, and is supported by selling vegetables and making coarse shoes. The shoemaker had protected the child for some weeks, and fed him gratis; but said that he could not keep him long, because he was too small to set upon the bench of his profession. "Well then, my little fellow," said the young gentleman, taking the boy by the hand, "I will get you a birth in the Almshouse, for I am too poor to keep you."

The cobbler and his wife came to the door with sad countenances. The frugal pair had potatoes to sell, and could make shift to live by the sweat of the brow. "I would gladly keep him," said the man, "but I have a large family, and he cannot earn any thing yet."

He was about to be led away to a sad place. "'Tis a pity," said the good woman, "that such a likely child should go to the poor-house: let him stay here."

It was concluded that the boy should remain where he was, until his mother was dead, or until a more eligible situation could be found.

The poor are frequently more beneficent than the rich: and the person, who of his penury gives all that he has, when duty demands it, shall be more honourable than those who give but a pittance from their luxuries, but two mites from their abundance. "It is more blessed to give than to receive."

JANUARY 21, 1813[8]

Early this morning, a sick man, W.F. sent for me to call at the Almshouse, and pray with him. Repeatedly I have visited him, but he is never weary of hearing the Gospel, and of uniting in prayer. This man, when young, was extravagantly fond of the theatre, and associated with lewd people there, so long, that he lost his health, and by the virulence of disease, his eyes. After he was thus visited for iniquity,[9] the

---

[8]Ely continued his ministry in 1812 but refrained from keeping a journal as he had become "weary with writing the history of human miseries." He resumed in 1813 as a way to provide an account to those who funded his efforts.

[9]*visited for iniquity:* struck with sickness on account of sinful living.

present place of his residence became his only home. Here he married one of the paupers, by whom he has a large family of children. He expresses much gratitude for my attentions to the welfare of his soul, and declares, that he desires complete sanctification from his sins, while his sole confidence for justification is reposed in Jesus Christ. This man I would not reproach with the past, which he deplores, but to the reader, I must say, that attachment to theatrical amusements took this person from all serious business, exposed him to strong temptations, and, in the issue, not only deprived him of sight, but made him the father of a numerous race of paupers. He was a man of no mean mental powers; but now he reposes in one of the lowest wards of the Almshouse, wears a long beard, is exposed to vermin, and is surrounded by every thing which is calculated to offend his remaining senses, and annihilate all hope for present life.

MARCH 9, 1813

... I went to a house in Henry-street, to instruct a sick and dying woman. In the third loft, the garret, I found the very person through whose habitation the wintry blast howls, and whose door is kept by famine. She has been feeble for years, and for five months has been unable to leave her bed. Her husband died of a fever in Havanna [sic], and left her, sick, and pennyless, to support two little children. One bed, one chair, and the half of another, one table, one candlestick, and a cup, an old pot, and the piece of a frying pan, is the complete inventory of her furniture. Her mother, an aged widow, spends the day with her, and in the night returns home; that is, to the house of another poor daughter, whose husband has marched with the army for Canada.[10]

MARCH 14, 1813

While I was preaching in the Hospital, this morning, an English seaman sat beside me, and wept continually. He has often discovered, on a similar occasion, the same feelings. It is difficult to form an opinion of him, for his character is that of a Christian, with one exception; he will, occasionally, drink intemperately. Formerly he became mad by intoxication; but ever since his recovery, deducting only a few weeks, he has been assistant-keeper in the Lunatic Asylum. No man is more faithful in the discharge of his duty, than he commonly is. No man seems to feel more

---

[10] As mentioned in the Library Committee report (Document 1) and the Society for the Prevention of Pauperism report (Document 2), the War of 1812 undermined the household economies of numerous families.

deeply than himself, the need a sinner stands in of the divine mercy. Few men appear to abhor the sin of drunkenness more thoroughly. He has been accustomed to drink nothing but his allowance of beer daily; and he has made many solemn promises to taste of no other liquor; but once in a few months he will enter the city to visit some friends, they will invite him to take another mug of ale, and then he has no sort of government of himself. He drinks until he can no longer stand. After a fit, his convictions and tears are renewed. He is haunted with extreme horrors, thinks himself lost, but will plead with God, almost continually for mercy. He confesses his transgressions, in a most humble manner, is fond of the Bible, and of public worship, and entreats that he may be locked up in one of the cells, when he is likely to become intemperate again. In short, he gives evidence that he is as much of a humble penitent, and sincere believer, as he can be; and yet occasionally have a drunken frolic. How invincible are those habits, which have, for a long time, been interwoven with the woof of our existence!

A drunkard and a Christian! It cannot be. Those names cannot subsist together in fellowship. . . .

9

The Boston Society for the Moral and Religious Instruction of the Poor

1819

Like Ezra Stiles Ely, Boston's Society for the Moral and Religious Instruction of the Poor looked upon working-class neighborhoods as rife with vice and ripe for conversion. Presuming that poverty was a function of individual sin, the male-run Boston Society equated missionary efforts with poor relief. "Associations are formed to relieve the daily wants of the sick, unfortunate, infirm, or aged," observed one of its annual reports, "but there are, we know, other wants than those of food, clothing, and shelter." By distributing tracts and Bibles and by guiding poor children into Sunday schools, the Boston Society hoped that spiritual salvation and economic uplift would go hand in hand.

Third Annual Report of the Boston Society for the Moral and Religious Instruction of the Poor, Presented at Their Anniversary, November 8, 1819 (Boston: U. Crocker, 1819).

RESPECTED INHABITANTS OF BOSTON,

You have seen, in the preceeding pages, what has been attempted for different classes of your townsmen; for seamen, for children of the poor, and for those, whom ignorance and vice have debarred from the blessings of that Christian community, in which a kind Providence has placed their lot. You will not refuse a hearty assent to the following propositions, which may be received with the confidence due to great moral and political axioms.

1. Among an ignorant and neglected population, the tendency to vice, crimes, poverty and wretchedness, is strong and rapid.

2. If this tendency be not checked, it not only destroys vast numbers by its direct influence, but endangers the peace and security of every member of society.

3. It is much wiser to prevent crimes by a salutary moral influence, than to rely solely upon punishment.

4. The mere dread of legal punishment never yet effectually deterred abandoned men from the perpetration of gross crimes.

5. But a judicious moral influence has saved multitudes from becoming abandoned; and has thus preserved society from numberless outrages, to which it would otherwise have been exposed.

6. Hence, a wise economy, and a regard to the protection and security of property, require, that the means of moral and religious instruction be furnished to all classes of the community, but especially to the poor.

7. Nine tenths of the pauperism in our country is occasioned by vice; and much the greater part of the public expenses for the support of the poor would be saved, if a great and general effort were made to instruct the ignorant, to encourage industry, and to restrain from the most noxious vices.

8. Under the influence of true benevolence and enlightened public spirit, the inhabitants of a large and wealthy town will provide, by private subscriptions and donations, if other means are not at hand, for the education of poor children, and the stated dissemination of religious truth.

With these things in view is it necessary to urge the claims of the Society, which now addresses you? Is there room for doubt, or hesitation, as to the point, whether the labors of this Society shall be extended, or suffered to languish for want of countenance and support? Rather let it be presumed, that the spontaneous and abundant liberality of the people of this ancient and opulent town will furnish ample means for carrying the benefits of instruction into every destitute neighborhood, and the comforts of industry, peace, and virtue to every fire-side.

10

Subjects of the New York House of Refuge
1825–1830

New York's Society for the Reformation of Juvenile Delinquents offered voyeuristic glimpses into the lives of youths hovering between poverty and criminality. Describing the escapades of fallen girls and abandoned boys, such accounts may have titillated or alarmed potential donors, and thus their formulaic presentations provide historians with insight regarding the preoccupations of middle-class Americans. These accounts—if read with a discerning eye—can also offer historians a greater understanding of the vagaries of a working-class childhood in the early republic: the transience and instability of families, the difficulties faced by the children of immigrant parents, the frequent shifting from household to household, the perils resulting from the death of a parent, and the scarcity of food, fuel, and work. Although these accounts were created as testaments to the power of New York's House of Refuge to redeem criminal children, we can use them to learn about children's economic contributions to household subsistence, their importance as workers in a range of industries, and their participation in an underground economy. Between 1825 and 1830, the House of Refuge received over 500 children, many of whom had been arrested for petty thefts.

January 1st, 1825—MARGARET SMITH, from the police, aged 13 years—born in New-York. Her father has been dead seven years. Her mother has since married a Mr. Smith, who left her mother last spring. She, by her mother's request, called herself Smith. Her father's name was Aaron McDoe. Her mother now lives in Banker-street; has lived there nearly two years; takes in washing, and goes out to work. Margaret has lived with Caleb Coggeshall five years; left there more than a year since, because they were not able to keep two persons, and she was too small to do all their work. She then lived seven months with Capt. Morgan, when they gave up house-keeping, and she then returned to

Examination of Subjects Who Are in the House of Refuge in the City of New-York (Albany: Croswell and Van Benthuysen, 1825); *Documents Relative to the House of Refuge, Instituted by the Society for the Reformation of Juvenile Delinquents in the City of New-York in 1824* (New York: Mahlon Day, 1832).

her mother. She used to pick chips,[1] and play in the streets;—was taken up at the theatre, with others. She has been at school to Mrs. Coggeshall. Enters 5th class.[2]

January 1st, 1825—JOHN BEEKMAN, aged 15 years July, 1824—born in New-York. His father, John, lives in Pike-street; is ship-rigger. His mother died nine years since. Father married twice since. He was put to live with Mr. Bull at Newburgh, where he stayed two weeks; then on board the sloop *Sportsman* two months; then through part of Pennsylvania; to Baltimore, to Harrisburgh, to Carlisle, to Philadelphia, Trenton, New-Brunswick, to New-York; all of which places he worked some time. He had no particular home; strayed about the streets; was taken up for stealing a pistol, and sent here. He has been in the almshouse; was bound from there, but did not stay over four months; has been to school; enters the 3d class.

January 1st, 1825—CATHARINE ANN ARMENTA, from the police, aged 15 years 1st May 1824—born in Pike-street. Her father has been dead eight years. Her mother lives in Pike-street; is a segar maker; she made segars with her mother; has lived at service with Mr. Bostwick, a boat-builder, six months; used to pick chips for her mother, and play in the street. She was taken up at the theatre in company of others, for stealing a watch; but she does not know any thing about it. Catharine has, it is believed, been acquainted with men. She has been 3 months to No. 2 school; to none other, except Sunday school. She enters the 2d class.[3]

January 11th, 1825—WILLIAM LABAYTEAUX RIKEMAN, from the police, aged 16 years—born in New-York. His father died five months since; he was a wood inspector. His mother lives on the corner of Pike and Lombardy-streets. She is almost blind; has two sisters that support his mother; has four brothers, two younger than himself, now with his

---

[1] *pick chips:* gather wood scraps to use for fuel.

[2] Residents of the House of Refuge spent one hour in the morning and one hour in the evening studying. Those in the fifth class learned "words and sentences from Scripture of two syllables."

[3] Catharine Armenta twice tried to escape from the House of Refuge, which house officials attributed to "the example of a depraved mother and elder sister, who are now in the Penitentiary." Physicians in the house were successful in medicating Catharine for epileptic fits. By the end of 1825, officials had "flattering hopes of her yet becoming a respectable woman."

mother. His father put him to Mr. Youle's furnace at Egg-harbor, where he stayed five months; he then returned, and stayed at home six months; did but little; played about the streets. He then went to live with Mr. George Hopper, a cooper, on trial; he stayed six months, and returned home, and worked some times in stave yards;[4] has often been sent to school, but used to play truant. To No. 2 school he thinks he was 18 months, but played truant more than half the time; has been to other schools but played truant. . . .

January 11th, 1825 — JOHN MULLIGAN, from the police, aged 14 years 17th March, 1824 — born in Philadelphia. Father has been dead four years. His mother since married to Moses Isaacs, who has gone to London. His mother lives in North Fourth-street, Philadelphia. She takes in sewing for a living. Not long after his mother married to Mr. Isaacs, he moved to Weehawken, where he was employed with his patent horse-boat.[5] He lived there about one year, and then returned to Philadelphia. Soon after the return, his mother put him to live with Peter Snyder, a tailor, where he lived from six to eight months, and then returned home. A few weeks after, he went to live with Mr. Duncan, an iron-monger, where he lived about six weeks, when he ran away and came to New-York about two months since; has been in prison in Philadelphia twice, for, as they say, stealing shoes, which he says he did not take. His motive in coming to New-York was to get a situation to go to sea. On his arrival, he took lodgings wherever they might be found. The first money that he got in New-York was at the theatre, when he picked a gentleman's pockets of $27. He says that was the only theft he committed in New-York. He continued to walk about the streets, boarded at any tavern, had no particular one; was taken up by Mr. Hays without any cause, and sent to Bridewell, where he was three or four days before he was sent here. He enters 5th class.

January 12th, 1825 — MARY ANN CORBITT, from the police, aged 15 years 17th December, 1824 — born in New-York. Father has been dead 14 years; mother has been dead five years. After the death of her mother, she went to Westchester, and lived with her grandmother, Mary Ann Bowers, where she lived four months; then returned and

---

[4]*stave yards:* lumberyards where planks were cut for making barrels.
[5]*patent horse-boat:* a boat either towed by a horse on shore or powered by a horse turning a paddle-wheel.

lived with Mr. Quick in the Bowery; then with Mr. Weyon, a baker, in Henry-street, 2½ years; then her grandmother came to town to live, and she went to stay with her, where she stayed about three months; then to Mrs. Fowler's in Lombardy-street; then to her aunt, Elizabeth Bowers, No. 100 Banker-street, which she has made her home since her mother's death. She has lived with Ezra Weeks, in Hudson-street, 3½ months; has lived with Mrs. Fowler three or four times, and with some others for a short time, sometimes one week and sometimes two weeks in a place; has played in the streets some; has seen considerable bad company; never ran about the streets night; she has been with her aunt, who lives in Banker-street, off and on for one year; she (her aunt) had no particular way of living; was sometimes drunk. She does not know what she was taken up for, unless it was to please her aunt. She does not think that it was her aunt's intention that she should come to this place. She enters the fifth class.[6]

September, 1827 — M.K., from the Commissioners, aged 12 years the first of April; born in Ireland. Her father and mother are both dead. Between three and four years since, her father, E.K. put her to live with Mr. J.P., a distiller, in this city, where she continued until within a few days since, when Mr. P. informs me that one of his hired men made free with her twice, the last time it was discovered by the servant woman: and as the child was young and had no friends, Mr. P. was fearful she would go to destruction, if she was not secured more closely than lay in his power; consequently obtained legal permission to send her here.

The girl simply states, that some weeks since, S., one of Mr. P's men, threw her on the floor, &c., and that a few days since, he found her in the still house, and threw her on the hogshead,[7] but the servant woman came so soon that he did not effect his purpose. She appears perfectly honest in her confession, says she never stole any thing; and I think if placed in a small careful family, will yet make a good girl to work.

January 9th, 1828 — S.H.L., from the Police, aged fourteen years the 25th of December; born in New-York. Her father is infirm and does no work, drinks hard — had a handsome property left him by his father, but has spent it. He was the cause of introducing his children to sell

[6]According to her teachers, Mary Ann Corbitt "appears determined upon becoming a respectable woman. She has acquired the art of manufacturing grass into hats, and has a happy faculty of teaching others."
[7]*hogshead:* a large cask or barrel.

soap and the like. . . . This little girl commenced her career about two years since, selling soap, needles, pencils, almanacs, &c. She first commenced to steal soap from Mr. H., then needles from Mr. P. in Maiden-lane—she has taken four hundred at a time; and would receive from her companions a part of their stolen property, and in turn would give them part of hers. I judge her not to be much past twelve years of age. She however learnt the trick of getting money from men, with the promise that she would go with them, and afterwards run away: her suitors would sometimes chase her; if she found herself too closely pursued, she would run into a grocery store, and tell them that a man was chasing her. She would pick up her sweethearts at the Battery, Steam Boat Wharves, Theatres, &c. She and her associates would occasionally attend the theatres and circuses. If they took five dollars each, per day, home to their mother, she was satisfied, and they could spend the rest. Sometimes they could clear eight dollars per day, honest sales, then again 12 per day, when they were successful in stealing needles and soap. . . .

1829—A.T., had been employed in selling sweet potatoes, clams, &c. about the streets, (the most fatal business a boy can pursue) and contracted the inveterate habit of drinking ardent spirits, which led to the commission of other errors. He was sent to the House as a vagrant. After 18 months of detention his conduct became so satisfactory, that he was indentured to learn a carpenter's trade. Poor fellow! his unhappy propensity returned upon him, and the slave of rum again became an inmate of the House of Refuge. Eighteen months training in temperate, industrious, and moral habits, had not been sufficient to cure that dreadful malady, and his master with sorrow gave him back to our care. After a suitable time had elapsed, he was bound out to a Nantucket Merchant, and departed on a three years whaling voyage. His letter dated "Coast of Japan, Lat. 32, Long."—is too long for insertion, but from its clear appearance and fair hand, we should judge that he was kept from the use of ardent spirits.[8]

1830—F.G.H., from the Commissioners of the Alms House, aged 13 years the 10th of September last, born in New-York of American parents. Her father was a ship carpenter by trade; died about three years

---

[8]In its first ten years, the House of Refuge sent over 180 boys on whaling voyages out of New Bedford or Nantucket. These lengthy trips subjected the young men to the harsh discipline and strenuous labor of the ship but allowed them to see the world on voyages that regularly traversed the Cape of Good Hope.

ago. Not long after, her mother commenced keeping a bad house in R. street, but removed to L. street, where after this course for nearly three years, she died, leaving three orphan daughters. This and the next youngest, about 11 years of age were taken charge of by the girls of ill fame, where the Commissioners found them about a week after her mother's death. The youngest, about seven years of age, was taken possession of by her mother's washer-woman. When she first came here, she was very wild, exhibiting that kind of deportment, which was natural for her to acquire from the examples of lewd girls.

September 17th, 1830—A.B., from the Police, aged 14 years the 22d of December last; born in New-York, of Irish parents. His father is an old porter; he occasionally drinks too much; then, the boy says his father will swear off for a year at a time, but when the time is past will pay for all in excess of drinking.

He has two sisters and one brother. A. and one of his sisters lived about two years in Paterson, where he was a good boy; but his father took him home to go to school, when he soon commenced playing truant and going round the markets (Washington and Fulton) stealing fruit.

He commenced, in junction with two others, stealing eggs from barrels standing by grocery stores, in which they were very successful, and one would pass and take a handful, and another would receive them at a convenient place, and sell them to a woman who kept a victualing stand, by the name of ——, who gave them one shilling for eighteen eggs. This woman would give them three shillings per piece for smoked beef, and from four to eight shillings for hams by the lump; these articles, this boy and his companions were very successful in stealing. He stole hats occasionally, sometimes they stole cocoa-nuts from stands and vessels, lead frequently, and sometimes old rope; but his associates told him that was too low, that he could make more at more honorable stealing. He once stole an umbrella in Maiden-lane, once he stole from the pocket of a drunken man three shillings, and at another time one shilling and eleven-pence from a money drawer in Hudson-street.

He was very successful in selling stolen handkerchiefs about the markets: they frequently stole clothes when they would be out to dry. A. was in the act of stealing a pair of pantaloons from a yard near the white fort, North River, when he was detected, taken and sent here. He would be frequently away from home, first one night, then a week and three weeks at a time, sleeping in shavings in new buildings, lumber yards, &c.

He and his companions had curious names for different articles that they stole, so as not to be understood by honest men: for instance: smoked beef or hams were smokers, hats cadies, shoes and boots crabs, handkerchiefs wipers, vests garvises, trowsers kickers, watches thimbles, shirts and other articles taken from yards were gooseberries; when they proposed to get articles of this kind, they would say we will go a gooseberrying; crockery and glass from crates would be tapping crates, a trunk they called Peter. They often deposited their goods in lumber yards and slept in them. He often went to the Theatre.

By the above, we see that this unfortunate, interesting boy, had learned many lessons in one year, and was in the broad road to destruction. On re-examination, the boy thinks it likely that he stole many other things; that he cannot remember all. Enters 6th class—could not read in the New Testament.[9]

[9]Appropriate for someone of this child's verbal dexterity, A. was bound out to a printer, where he learned to set type.

11

Letter to Graduates of the House of Refuge
1829

The capstone of the House of Refuge's rehabilitation program was to send urban children as far from the city as possible. The institution sent girls into rural New York as domestic servants. Boys might end up on a whaling ship in the Pacific Ocean or in the Ohio countryside as a farmhand. Before setting off to their new homes, these apprentices received a special document from the managers of the Society for the Reformation of Juvenile Delinquents. Intended to remind the children of lessons learned in the House of Refuge, this form letter attested to the early republic's growing faith in the self-made individual. The belief that economic success and moral sinlessness were essentially matters of free choice would prove important in broader debates over public welfare and the causes of poverty.

Fourth Annual Report of the Society for the Reformation of Juvenile Delinquents in the City of New-York (New York: Mahlon Day, 1829).

To *[child's name here]*:

You are about to leave the House of Refuge. You will be bound as an apprentice to a person, who, the Managers believe, will provide for you, instruct you, and if you behave well, treat you with kindness.

We should not have consented to part with you at this time, had not your conduct given us reason to hope, that the religious and moral instruction you have received, since you have been under our care, have disposed you to lead an honest, industrious, and sober life. You are now of an age when you are capable of distinguishing between virtue and vice; you have had experience that must teach you, that if you are good you may be happy, if you are bad you must be miserable. You can not but have perceived how much your welfare depends upon yourself, and upon the observance of precepts you have seen inculcated with so much pains by your preceptors in the House of Refuge. Among these are the following:—You are always to tell the truth. You are to be obedient to those under whose care you are placed, doing your duty as well as you know how, industriously and cheerfully. You are to be civil and respectful in your manners, and to avoid all bad language. You will find time that you may employ, not only in religious reading and exercises, but in improving your mind, and in acquiring such learning as may be useful to you. If you mean to be a good and respectable man, you will not fail to avail yourself of these opportunities.

Do not be discouraged by what has happened from striving to raise yourself to a respectable station in the world. If your life be hereafter exemplary, the errors of your infancy will be forgiven or forgotten. In our happy country, every honest man may claim the rewards he merits. Many of our most distinguished citizens have been the makers of their own fortunes, and in their childhood were as poor and unprotected as you have been. There is no reason why you, if you pursue the course they have done, may not command the same good fortune. At all events, you may be sure, that if you make yourself master of your business, are diligent in your calling, establish a character, for truth, honesty, industry, and sobriety, you can not fail to obtain a comfortable living, and to be beloved and respected. Look at those you have seen in poverty, and observe those you will hereafter meet with, who are in want: you will generally, if not always, find that they owe their condition to bad company, to idleness, and intemperance, which not only debase the individual, but often make all who have the misfortune to be connected with him, unhappy and ashamed to acknowledge any relationship.

Figure 4. *House of Refuge.*
Following the lead of New York and Boston, Philadelphia opened its own House of Refuge in 1827. Within a few years, the institution sheltered 100 children at a time, indenturing most of them to employers beyond the city limits. This emblem suggests the institution's power to transform dirty street urchins into upstanding youth of promise.
Cephas G. Childs, *House of Refuge, Philadelphia.* Print Collection, Miriam and Ira D. Wallach Division of Art, Prints and Photographs, The New York Public Library, Astor, Lenox and Tilden Foundations.

When you see a man, and particularly a young man, frequenting bad company, given to drink, and using profane language; when you see that he neglects his business, is wasting his time, and taking no pains to learn, you may be sure he is in the road to ruin; he has no chance to be reputable; he can hope for nothing but to live all his days from hand to mouth, and to earn by mean and hard bodily labor, enough to keep himself alive, and if he should have a family, to keep them from starving. On the other hand, if you see a young man attentive to his business, passing his leisure time soberly, but cheerfully, with companions of whom he need not be ashamed; if he loses no opportunity of gaining religious and moral instruction, and is obedient and civil in his manners, you may be sure that when left to make his own way in the world, he will always be beforehand. Instead of leading a life of continual toil and hardship, and of reliance on his daily labor for his daily bread, he will become independent and happy, and may have around him a family and friends who will esteem and respect him, and be proud of their connection with one who is so deserving.

You well know the evil consequences of bad company: there is nothing as to which you ought to be more on your guard. You ought particularly to avoid those with whom you associated before you [were] placed in the House of Refuge. That you may not be again tempted by these, you should not be too anxious to return to this city, and put yourself in a situation where you may meet with them. When your time of service is out, and you become your own master, you have a better chance of success in the world, if you will establish yourself where you will have no friends but those you may hereafter make by your good conduct, and where the history of your early life is unknown.

It shall always be gratifying to us to hear of your welfare. We shall be pleased to learn that you preserve and often read this letter. We wish you occasionally to write to our Superintendent; you will always find in him, and in us, friends ready to advise and serve you.

Committing you to the protection of Providence, and to the care of your master, and repeating our admonition to you, to be religious, to love the truth, to be sober and industrious, and to avoid bad company, we bid you farewell.

12

Subjects of the
New York Colored Orphan Asylum
1837–1838

The self-made ethic had limited applicability to the lives of poor African American children. Excluded from the House of Refuge, unlikely to receive apprenticeships in desirable trades, and ultimately denied full civil rights in their adulthoods, impoverished African American children had little prospect of upward mobility. Nor could they count on other sources of private relief. Urban black communities generally lacked the financial resources to erect asylums. Although an increasing number of white philanthropists were focusing their attention on the abolition of slavery in the South, charity efforts on behalf of free African Americans in the North were scanty. New York's Colored Orphan Asylum, however, did provide a sanctuary to black children whose families had lost the ability to maintain them. The children who entered the Colored Orphan Asylum were frequently sick, debilitated by exposure, malnutrition, and dangerous labor. Although these brief biographies of the institution's earliest residents are particularly bleak (and fraught with the racial and class assumptions of the white writers who penned them), they reveal the chronic vulnerability of African American children in a society structured upon slavery and white supremacy.

ELIZABETH JACKSON, aged 7, born in Patterson NJ in 1829. Her mother who was named Mary Jackson was originally a slave, but was freed by the laws of the state of New Jersey. She died two or three years before Elizabeth's admission to the asylum. Her father's name is unknown. She was living at the time of her admission with her grandparents. An orphan girl, was met by one of the Managers last winter in Madison-street, having been sent for liquor by her grandmother. The wretchedness of the place from which she was taken can hardly be surpassed. When called for at mid-day, she was found in bed with scarcely a

Second Annual Report of the Association for the Benefit of Colored Orphans (New York: Mahlon Day, 1838); *Third Annual Report of the Association for the Benefit of Colored Orphans* (New York: Mahlon Day, 1839); "Association for the Benefit of Colored Orphans Admissions Records, 1837–1840," MSS, New-York Historical Society.

vestige of clothing. With the assistance of a few articles hastily procured, she was dressed and carried to the Asylum. She proved to be a child of untractable [*sic*] temper, and feeble intellect, the result probably of a diseased brain. Evident improvement was however observed in her character and deportment, and when the managers witnessed her death a few months after her admission, it was not without the hope, that her spirit, renewed and sanctified by divine grace, had passed from ignorance and degradation to a world of purity and happiness.

JOHN TOMATA, [aged 8 or 9] an orphan boy, born in slavery in the West Indies. He was brought by his mistress from Havana to this city, and here voluntarily emancipated. When admitted, he was suffering from disease of the spine and to those who saw him for the first time, his sadly expressive countenance and the distressing infirmity under which he labored, made a most touching appeal. It was hoped that the spinal affliction might be arrested, but the approach of cold weather developed consumptive symptoms, which proved ultimately fatal. His disposition was grateful and uncomplaining, and always readily responsive to the slightest expression of interest or sympathy. During the last few painful hours which preceded his death he was frequently heard to exclaim in mournful tones, "no father, no mother." He had learned nothing of the English language except a few broken sentences. . . .

JOHN ROSAL, admitted June 1837, born November 1829. His father whose name was John Rosal died in New York, Jan. 16th, 1837. His mother Diana Rosal died November 25th, 1836. The character of his parents is said to have been of the most vicious and degraded kind. After the death of John Rosal's mother, his father who had taken no care of his wife or child for a long time abandoned him entirely. A coloured woman named [illegible] of very respectable character, who lived in the upper part of the house where his mother died, took charge of him. This woman brought him to the Asylum. John Rosal is said to have a grandmother residing in Hackensack (NJ) who is a respectable woman with some property. . . .

CINDERELLA JACKSON, admitted November 1837, was born in New York, December 25th, 1828. Her mother, Maria Jackson died of consumption, September 15th, 1837. Her father John Jackson also died of consumption in the latter part of March 1835. Cinderella was brought to the Asylum by her step father, Isaac Wright. He has been a labourer in the employ of Addison, Willmarth, and Co. . . . He is in bad health and speaks of some articles of clothing and furniture, and perhaps a little money to which she will be entitled on his death. . . .

JACOB BECKET LEE was admitted October 10th, 1837, born at the South probably in 1829. His mother Maria Lee died of cholera in New York in 1833. His father—Lee was a fugitive slave from Virginia and was apprehended by his master in New York and carried back to slavery. He was brought to the Asylum by a friend of his mother named Comfort Becket living in Walnut Street. Jacob B. Lee was apprenticed to Thomas H. Thomas of New York, as a house-servant on the 19th of April, 1839. His term of apprenticeship will expire on the 19th of April 1850.[1]

JEREMIAH RAWLE, born (probably) in 1829, and Adeline Rawle, born (probably) 1831, admitted November 20th, 1837. Jeremiah and Adeline Rawle are the children of Minerva Rawle, a slave in the state of Virginia, who was liberated under the will of her master. Rawle, together with about forty others, who removed to New York in the autumn of 1837. They were all in destitute circumstances at the time of their arrival, and these children, appearing to be proper subjects for the Asylum, were with the consent of their mother brought there, not long after their arrival. Their mother was a vicious and ignorant woman, and from her ungovernable temper became exceedingly troublesome to the inmates of the Asylum. She died in the summer of 1839. Their father is believed to be still living in slavery in Virginia.[2]

HARRISON NICHOLS, born in 1835, and Charles Nichols, born in 1833, admitted November 1838. The mother of Charles and Harrison Nichols died of scarlet fever about fourteen months before they were brought to the Asylum. Her name was Susan. Their father, a worthy man, went to sea soon after the death of his wife and has since not been heard of. They were taken care of until brought to the Asylum by a relative named Lucinda Dunham, who being unable to maintain them any longer, carried them to the Police office, whence they were sent to the Asylum. She lives at No 48 Third Str in the rear and appears to be a worthy woman.

[1] Jacob Lee ran away after one year.
[2] Jeremiah Rawle was apprenticed to Caroline Teller of Fishkill Landing in Dutchess Co. and presented with some land afterward. Adeline Rawle was apprenticed as a house-servant, but her new mistress died and Adeline returned to the Asylum until her eighteenth birthday.

Public Institutions

13

Rules for the Government of the New York Almshouse

1801

New York City had long offered indoor relief to the poor. Its first alms-house was constructed in 1736, and sixty years later, it housed nearly 800 men, women, and children — twice the building's capacity. The city built a new almshouse in 1797, using funds raised through a public lottery. The new facility stood near City Hall, which brought the institution constant scrutiny. Almshouse officials and the city council worked to maintain order and to establish administrative procedures for dressing, housing, and feeding the poor. At the time of this report, few Americans believed that almshouses could redeem the character of the poor. More likely, mismanagement and permissive government would result in the corruption of innocent women and children. As a result, almshouse administrators focused much of their attention on segregating the poor by sex, color, age, and character.

... The design of the institution is to provide for the comfortable maintenance of such paupers as are unable to gain subsistence by labor, and have either no legal settlement in the city, or no other legal provision for their support.

Rules for the Government of the Alms-House in the City of New-York, Approved and Agreed to at a Common Council, on Monday, the Sixth Day of October, 1800 (New York: Furman and Loudon, 1801).

Hence it appears that those who are able to maintain themselves by industry, are not the primary objects of the institution—where such persons are unwilling to work, they cannot be, in any point of view, objects of public charity; and instead of being supported in idleness, they are to be corrected by the vigilance of the police. Where, on the contrary, the poor have strength and inclination to labor for their subsistence, they are entitled to encouragement and reward; and in our country (the price of labor being high and employment plenty) they generally receive it. Instances, however, may occur, where employment may be wanting; and in all such cases, suitable work should be furnished to the applicants, either at home, or in some other public rooms, where they might receive a portion of their pay in good and wholesome food, for themselves and their families.

Excluding, therefore, from this institution, all those classes of the poor, which are able to gain, by their industry, the means of subsistence, still it will necessarily contain persons of many different descriptions; some of them reduced to indigence, by disease and misfortune; others, whose wants are the effects of vice and intemperance; others again, in the last stage of life, bending under the weight of age and infirmities; and others, who in their infancy, have been thrown upon the public charity, for support and education. An institution, comprehending such a variety of characters, must be complicated in its nature, and subject to abuses, which it is difficult to remedy.

The chief ends to be pursued, and of which sight should never be lost—are,

I. The comfort and welfare of those who are dependent upon the public charity—and
II. The due administration of the funds appropriated to the support of the poor, by avoiding all unnecessary expence, and introducing a regular system of management and accounts.

The first of these general heads, includes all that relates to the classing, diet, cloathing, health and general treatment of the paupers; the education and binding out of the children, and the preservation of decency, sobriety, and cleanliness—the committee suppose that is of great importance,

1. That the different descriptions of paupers should be separated as far as possible, into different classes; and those whose lives have been uniformly virtuous, should not be confounded with persons of another character.

2. The practice of suffering persons of different sexes to live promiscuously in the same rooms, should, for the sake of decency and propriety, be carefully avoided.
3. The greatest attention should be paid to the cleanliness of the house, and of the persons of the paupers, and of the frequent airing of their rooms and bedding.
4. The diet of the paupers, should be palatable and nutritious, and served to them with regularity and neatness, at stated hours.
5. Such of the paupers as are capable of any work, should be furnished with it; and should receive a suitable compensation.
6. The sick, should in general, be separated from those who are in health.
7. A due sense of religion should be carefully inculcated, as the greatest comfort under temporal afflictions; and for this purpose, a few pious books might be furnished, divine service performed in the house as often as might be convenient, and such of the paupers as are capable, encouraged in reading to others.
8. Spirituous and strong liquors should be absolutely interdicted, unless when given by the advice of a physician.
9. The children of the house should be under the government of careful matrons—they should be uniformly dressed and lodged in separate apartments, according to their different sexes; they should be kept as much as possible from the other paupers, habituated to decency, cleanliness and order, and carefully instructed in reading, writing, and arithmetic. The girls should also be taught to sew and knit.
10. When the children arrive at proper ages, great care should be taken to furnish them with suitable places, that they may be instructed in some useful trade or occupation; and as the Commerce and Navy of the country are becoming of great importance, it would be well if there was a power of binding to the sea-service, when it should be judged most advantageous.

With regard to the second general head, viz. the due administration of the funds appropriated to the support of the poor, economy is the essential principle to be adopted, as far as may be consistent with the primary objects of the Institution. It is certain that the maintenance of the Poor in this City is, and for a long time has been, a heavy burden upon the citizens; perhaps the most weighty in the catalogue of their

Taxes. It is also to be expected, from the growing bulk and population of the Town, as well as from extraneous circumstances, that the burden, in its aggregate, will continue to increase. Hence a constant attention to the economy and order, in this important branch of the public expenditures, is a manifest and serious duty, which the Corporation owe to themselves and their constituents.

The public have an undoubted right to expect, that as they pay, and must continue to pay this heavy tax, it will be prudently expended and duly accounted for; which can only be effected by pursuing a regular system of management, and keeping fair and clear entries of all the transactions relating to the Alms-House.

In this view it will be necessary,

1. That great attention should be paid to the purchase of provisions, fuel, cloathing, medicines, and other necessaries for the House.
2. That the management and expenditure of these several articles, and particularly of the fuel, should be diligently guarded.

That regular accounts should be kept in the most perfect and systematic manner, of all purchases and expenditures of articles, and of all work done at the house, and that a clear and comprehensive state of the whole, should be exhibited to the Corporation at certain regular periods and at any other times when they may think proper to require it.

It must be obvious that the several points above stated under both the general heads, are of great importance, and it is far from improbable, that they are at present not so perfectly attended to as might be wished. This is not however mentioned, with a view of reflecting upon any of the persons concerned in the management of the Alms-House. The fault (if it exists) is more in the system than in the men. The doing of business by a board of commissioners, who serve without compensation, is at first view plausible, as it carries the appearance of economy, and evidences a disinterested zeal for the public service; but in practice this mode has seldom been successful; very little responsibility attaches to any of the commissioners. The burthen which no one in particular is bound to sustain, is shifted from shoulder to shoulder, till at last it is left wholly unsupported; and as no compensation is to be received, no one thinks himself bound to sacrifice his own private affairs, to an object of general concern, and which there are so many others equally engaged in. The committee, however, are convinced that the success of any plan, must after all, depend in a great measure, upon the persons who are to execute it. In every thing that relates to the affairs of the poor, a rare union of system, intelligence, talents and industry is requisite; and without such union as a judicious writer has observed, "Millions may be wasted without bettering their condition." In selecting therefore, the person who may be the chief conductor of the business, many difficulties will occur, and unless such a salary is allowed, as may command abilities, reward industry, and prevent the effect of small temptations, it is in vain to hope for any permanent advantages. . . .

14

Rules and Regulations of the Salem Almshouse

1816

Although almshouses were not penal institutions like jails or penitentiaries, they served a disciplinary purpose. Indeed, many localities tried to make their almshouses as inhospitable as possible to discourage the poor from living at the public's expense. Most almshouses regulated the waking hours of their inhabitants, mandating strenuous labor, stipulating a diet of bland food, and limiting opportunities for relaxation. The 1816 rules of the Salem, Massachusetts, almshouse were typical of early republic institutions.

Time of Rising and Public Worship. At the first ringing of the bell in the morning, every person, the sick and infirm excepted, must instantly rise, dress and repair to the Pumps and cleanse themselves; after which, if Sunday, they must put on their best apparel, and at the ringing of the bell, at a time which will be communicated to them, they must repair to the Chapel, and there behave with decency and sobriety; no noise or disturbance shall be allowed in any part of the house, and the day shall be strictly observed as set apart both from recreation and unnecessary labour, and any persons willfully absenting themselves from divine services, shall be subject to prompt and severe punishment.

Rules and Regulations for the Government of the Alms-House in Salem . . . December, 1816, broadside, American Antiquarian Society.

Meals. The bell will be rung 10 minutes before each Meal, when every person will cease from any occupation they may be engaged in, and be ready with clean hands and faces for the ringing of the second bell, when they will repair to the Mess-Rooms, and take such seats as shall be assigned to them by the keeper, where they must strictly observe decency and good order. Half an hour each will be allowed for Breakfast and Supper, and one hour for dinner, at the expiration of which times the bell will be again rung, when every person shall immediately repair to the work assigned them by the keeper. They shall not take any bread or other food with them; they shall not loiter on the way, but shall proceed with alacrity and at once commence their labour. No cooking whatever will be permitted in any room except the kitchen, nor shall any provisions be carried into any of the rooms, those occupied by the sick and infirm excepted.

Kitchen and Mess Rooms. The Kitchen and Mess Rooms, cooking utensils and furniture, are to be under the immediate care of the Chief Cook, who must keep them all perfectly clean; he must be punctual in preparing his Meals, prudent and careful of the provisions and wood entrusted to him, and see that nothing is wasted—and he shall carefully collect the fragments after meals, and preserve them for the Pigs, which are also under his care, and to feeding of which he must be attentive. Immediately after each meal he must clean the mess rooms and tables, and prepare them for the next meal. To aid in all which, necessary assistants will be assigned him, who must obey his directions; he must not suffer any idlers to be in the kitchen, nor deliver to any person, or allow to be taken any provisions out of the usual meal times, unless ordered by the keeper.

Cleanliness. Every tenanted Room in the House, together with the entries and stairways, must be swept clean every morning, and scoured once a week, or oftener if necessary, by such persons as the keeper shall appoint. No filth or dirt shall be thrown out of the windows, and no person shall in any way dirty the yards or out-houses, and the sweepings of the house shall be deposited by the sweepers in a place or places directed by the keeper.

Washing Day. On Sunday morning every person shall bundle their dirty cloaths together and place them in rooms which shall be assigned for that purpose, previously designating them by some proper mark, from whence on Monday morning they shall be taken by the washer women, appointed by the keeper, thoroughly washed, dried and bundled each by themselves, and placed in the rooms from whence they were taken, and no washing at any other time will be allowed unless by permission of the keeper.

Retirement for the Night. At 9 o'clock P.M. in Summer, and at 8 o'clock P.M. in Winter, on the ringing of the bell, every person in the house must repair to their apartment, extinguish the lights, secure the fires, and retire to bed.

Turnkey. The Turnkey must attend to the opening of the Gates, no visitors are to be admitted by him nor any person belonging to the house allowed to go out, without leave of the keeper. All visitors of a suspicious appearance, as well as tenants of the house, of the same description, shall be strictly searched, and if any ardent spirits shall be found upon them, the former shall be forever after refused admission to the house, and the latter confined in a cell.

Admission of Visitors. No visitors will be admitted to the house except on Wednesdays between 9 o'clock A.M. and 4 o'clock P.M. except the friends and relations of the sick, who may be admitted at other times by permission of the keeper. No money will be allowed to be presented to any inhabitant of the house, except through the hands of the keeper. The inhabitants of the house are strictly forbidden to beg either within or out of the house.

Tasks. Tasks shall be assigned by the keeper to all who are capable of labour, and those who perform them faithfully and cheerfully, shall be rewarded according to their merits by such indulgencies as the keeper shall deem expedient. No work whatever shall be performed by the inhabitants of the house out of the same for any citizen of the town.

Disorderly conduct and profane language. The severest punishment will be inflicted on all those who are guilty of drunkenness, disorderly conduct, profane or obscene language, theft embezzlement, waste of food or manufacturing stock, or any other waste whatever; and no rum or other ardent spirits, on any occasion, or under any pretence whatever, will be permitted to be brought into the house.

Solitary confinement. In all cases of solitary confinement for highly criminal conduct, the prisoner shall be debarred from seeing or conversing with any person whatever, except the keeper of the house and the person employed by him to supply to their wants, and they shall in all other respects be subject to the severest privations; their food shall consist solely of bread and water, and any inhabitant of the house, other than those excepted, who shall have any communication whatever with a person so confined, shall be subject to a like punishment. All persons confined to the cells must be previously searched, and every instrument taken from them.

Intercourse of the Sexes.   No communication whatever, except in cases specially authorised by the keeper, shall be allowed between the unmarried males and females belonging to the house, and all unlawful connection between the sexes is strictly prohibited—any violation of this rule shall subject the violator to the severest punishment.

Hospital.   The Nurses who take charge of the Hospital are exempt from all other duty; they shall keep the apartments, beds and bedding in perfect cleanliness, and shall at all times, by night and by day, pay every care and attention to the sick.

Burials.   Whenever a person dies in the house, the relatives or friends may remove the body and inter it at their own expence, otherwise it will be buried in the ground which now is or may hereafter be laid out for that purpose; the relations and friends of the deceased will be allowed to attend the funeral at the discretion of the keeper—and any unbecoming conduct will be punished.

School.   School hours shall be from 9 to 12 o'clock, A.M. and 2 to 4 o'clock, P.M. in the Winter, and from 8 to 11 o'clock, A.M. and 2 to 5 o'clock, P.M. in Summer, Sundays and the afternoons of Wednesdays and Saturdays excepted. . . .

Sick and infirm.   No person shall be considered sick and infirm so as to exempt them from labour, unless pronounced so by the attending Physician.

Punishments.   The keeper will be vigilant in detecting every negligence or wilful violation of these Rules, and will promptly inflict the most exemplary punishment—at the same time, those who conduct well will receive the kindest treatment, and every reasonable indulgence.

Figure 5. *Almshouse Labor.*

As public relief administrators sought to make the almshouse less attractive to the poor, they imposed physical labor upon inmates. While some almshouses employed paupers to assist in the daily operations of the facility and provided useful job training, other institutions devised more punitive approaches simply to prove that the needy must earn their bread through the sweat of their brows. Picking oakum (disentangling old ropes into individual strands) was a common task, but New York and Philadelphia set paupers climbing on a treadmill.

Stephen Allen, *Reports on the Stepping or Discipline Mill, at the New York Penitentiary: Together with Several Letters on the Subject* (New York: Van Pelt and Spear, 1823). This item is reproduced by permission of The Huntington Library, San Marino, California.

15

The Boston House of Industry

1821

While serving in the Massachusetts legislature, Josiah Quincy (1772–1864) led a committee studying poor-relief practices throughout the state. The 1821 Quincy Report criticized out-relief programs as expensive and morally harmful. In contrast, it recommended workhouses to preserve "the industrious habits" of the poor. Workhouses promised cost savings by discouraging the poor from seeking support but also by turning a profit on inmate labor. Quincy's hometown of Boston (which would soon elect him mayor) immediately seized on the House of Industry to reduce its expenditures on poor relief. In the following report, Boston reformers argued that requiring the poor to work would "repress the mischievous effects of that weak and listless sensibility, miscalled benevolence, which scatters its bounty without discrimination."

. . . [The committee has] examined the state of the present Town Alms House and compared it with institutions of a similar character, in this vicinity, particularly with those at Marblehead and Salem,[1] and they are unanimously of opinion that the accommodations, provided for the poor, at the Alms House, in Boston, are not such as comport with the honor and interests of the Town. They are also unanimously of opinion that, in aid of the present establishment, a work house, to be denominated, a House of Industry, should be erected, with a sufficient quantity of land attached to it, so as to enable the poor, compelled to resort to it, to have the benefit resulting from air, employment and exercise, and the town to derive that advantage, which other towns in this vicinity experience from the well directed labour of the poor, in similar institutions. . . .

In forming this opinion, your committee were influenced by considerations of economy;—the strong conviction that a great saving would in consequence, result to the town, in point of expense;—and above all, by a sense of the salutary influence of a well managed institution of

[1] *Marblehead, Salem:* nearby Massachusetts cities.

Report of the Committee on the Subject of Pauperism and a House of Industry of the Town of Boston (Boston: n.p., 1821).

this kind on the public morals. The obligations, which every society owes to those classes of citizens, which are liable to become pensioners on its charity, were not overlooked, in making this estimate of the Town's interest and duty.

There are four classes of persons, to which the public arrangements, on these subjects, ought to extend, and to whose peculiarities of condition they ought, as far as any general system is practicable, to be accommodated;—1st, the poor, by reason of age;—2d, the poor, by reason of misfortune;—3d, the poor, by reason of infancy—4th, the poor, by reason of vice.

It is very plain, that each of these classes of poor have claims upon society, differing both in their nature and degree, founded upon different principles; the sources of different duties, and requiring different proportions of sympathy and solicitude.

Of all classes of the poor, that of virtuous old age, has the most unexceptionable claims upon society; and is that, in relation to which its charitable establishments should be so constructed as to extend, not only comfort, but a reasonable degree of indulgence. This cause of helplessness cannot successfully be feigned. It is the consequence of a general law of our nature, to which all are equally liable. Hope and pleasure are, for this life, in a great measure extinguished. Its condition requires, therefore, a peculiar degree of consideration. Although the old, should not wholly be excused from labour, yet it is apparent that such ought to be provided as is suited to their age; if possible to their habits and former employments in life.

A similar course of remark applies to those, who are helpless, through corporeal, or intellectual misfortune;—the effect of no vice, nor criminal indulgence. Each of these classes is entitled to particular consideration; neither should be released from every degree and kind of labour, yet what is required should be adapted to their condition, and their particular imbecility. Something more of attention should be paid, and of pains taken, to gratify their inclinations and to supply their humble wants.

Now the impracticability of making this first and great discrimination, in favour of these two first classes of poor, is the great defect of the Boston Alms House. In an establishment so restricted in point of room; and open to the indiscriminate influx of characters of all descriptions, it is impossible to make those distinctions, either in food, or in treatment, which is due to age and misfortune.

If the aged and virtuous poor are reduced to the food, and made obnoxious to the severity, or the labour, to which the vicious are subjected, it is to them a degradation, and a new and undeserved source of misery and misfortune. On the other hand, if the vicious are permitted to enjoy the comforts, or partake of the indulgence, which is due to age and misfortune, their condition becomes, not only supportable, but eligible.[2] The fear of poverty is diminished, and the shame of dependence obliterated. Public establishments become thronged; as will never fail to be the case, whenever Alms House support is better than, or even equal, in its kind, to the support to be obtained by labour. These considerations, and others, which will readily present themselves to the reflections of intelligent men, render it indispensable that an establishment should be provided, which should enable the Town to make this first, most important, and just of all discriminations between the poor, in consequence of vice; and the poor, in consequence of misfortune.

The third class, consisting of those, who are poor, and in infancy or childhood, are somewhat differently situated; and have a right to require from society a distinct attention and more scrupulous and precise supervision. Their career of existence is but just commenced. They may be rendered blessings, or scourges to society. Their course may be happy or miserable, honourable or disgraceful, according to the specific nature of the provision, made for their support and education. It follows that the charitable establishments of every wise and virtuous community ought to be such as to enable it to effect these interesting objects, in the most perfect and satisfactory manner.

The present condition of the Boston Alms House, precludes all possibility of extending that free air, exercise, and healthful labour, and of attaining that separation from the contamination of vicious language and example, which is requisite and due to this class. Intimately connected with this topic is that of providing for those idle and vicious children, of both sexes and different ages, which often under the command, and always with the permission of thoughtless and abandoned parents, are found begging in our streets, or haunting our wharves, or market places, sometimes under the pretence of employ, at others for the purpose of watching occasions to pilfer small articles, and thus beginning a system of petty stealing; which terminates often in the gaol; often in the penitentiary; and not seldom, at the gallows.

Power enough already exists, in the hands of the constituted authorities, and if it do not, might easily be obtained, to rid ourselves of this nuisance, and to place these unfortunate children under either

---

[2] *eligible:* desirable.

a system of discipline, or of restraint; or of useful labour. At present, however, this is absolutely impracticable. There is no place, suitable for their reception. The present Alms House is insufficient for its present tenants; more it is impossible to accommodate. A work house, or house of industry, is, therefore, absolutely essential, previously to taking any steps for the improvement of this unhappy, and abandoned class, of children. On this point, your committee do not apprehend that any thing more forcible can be added, to make the essential nature of such an establishment as that, which they recommend, apparent and unquestionable.

The fourth class, the poor by reason of vice, constitute, here, and every where, by far the greater part of the poor; amounting always, probably to a full two thirds of the whole number of the adult poor. As it is for these, that the proposed house of industry is intended, in its first operations, to provide, the present seems a proper occasion to explain the general views of your committee in relation to this establishment; and to what objects and plans those views, at present, and to what they ultimately extend. Indolence, intemperance, and sensuality, are the great causes of pauperism, in this country. Notwithstanding the imbecility induced by their habits and vices, it is yet found by experience, that generally speaking, all of this class can do something; and very many of them a great deal; and some of them fall little, and often not at all, short of the ability to perform, daily, the complete task of a day labourer.

The present accommodations of the Boston Alms House, not furnishing the means, nor the space for actual employ, their labour is but little, and of small account. The course of practice of this class is, to come, or to be brought to the Alms House in a state of disease, or intoxication, or, in the winter, in actual want, and after passing weeks, or months, crowded together, within its walls; after being cured, restored and supported, during sickness and through inclement seasons, they are permitted to depart; to enter upon the same career of vice and indulgence, until they are brought back again; to be again supported and cured; and again sent forth to commence and pursue the same circle. Now, it is apparent, that so long as this class can come when they will, and depart when they will,—so long as Alms House fare is upon a level, in point of quality and comfort, and often a little superior to their out-of-door support and comforts,—so long as little, or no, work is required of them, within the walls, and there is no land belonging to the establishment, on which they can work, without,—that they have little, or no inducement either to labour or to economize, in order to prevent their being compelled to resort to it: on the contrary, it is obvious that the certainty of a comfortable and easy life, in the winter, is a perpetual and very effectual encouragement to a thoughtless, dissipated and self-indulgent course in the summer. Accordingly institutions of this kind, when from necessity, or any other circumstances, they are conducted upon such principles, may justly be considered as encouraging and augmenting the amount of pauperism in a community. It follows, therefore, from these considerations, that it is the great duty of every society to take care that their Alms Houses should be provided with space of land and accommodations, to enable those, who have the superintendance of them to provide work for this class; and for every class in it, according to its ability; to the end that they should never become the resort of idleness, for indulgence; nor of vice, for comfort; nor of disease, for cure, without cost. . . .

16

Inmates of the Baltimore Almshouse

June 1825

When needy Baltimore residents entered the city's almshouse, the clerk entered their names into a massive leather book. In hopes of developing a better understanding of the causes of urban poverty, the institution's administrators surveyed each entrant about age, birthplace, duration of residence in Baltimore, religion, malady, occupational skills, and tobacco use. Although impoverished men and women may have told scintillating tales of their travels and exploits, the data entered into the admissions book was so standardized as to mute the teller's voice. Instead, the clerk holding the pen was able to distill an entire life into shorthand that reduced lived experience to only a few salient categories. Nonetheless, the entries for the forty-three people who arrived at the almshouse in June 1825 present a demographic profile of early republic failure and desperation.

"Baltimore Almshouse Admissions and Discharge Book," MS 1866.1, Manuscripts Department, Maryland Historical Society Library.

OTTER CAST
Occupation: gravedigger
Admitted: June 6, 1825   Exit: died in the Almshouse
                                September 16, 1825
Malady: crazy from drink

PHILIP LEE, 48
Birth: 1777, Harford County, Maryland
Residence: lived in Baltimore since 1800
Occupation: currier   Religion: Methodist
Admitted: June 6, 1825   Exit: died in the Almshouse
                                November 15, 1825
Malady: consumption   Other: uses tobacco
Previous Stint: August 30, 1824 to May 26, 1825 (discharged)

ELIZABETH WOLCOTT, 23
Birth: 1802, Virginia
Residence: lived in Baltimore since 1824
Occupation: housework
Admitted: June 6, 1825   Exit: discharged July 5, 1825
Malady: pregnant by Wm. Founham, who has no residence

WILLIAM CARROLL, 8
Birth: 1817, Baltimore
Admitted: June 7, 1825   Exit: bound out as apprentice
                                July 18, 1825
Malady: deserted by his father, William James Carroll, a 33 year-old
Irish Catholic weaver who had arrived in Baltimore in 1814. William
James Carroll had brought four of his children into the Almshouse in
January 1824. His daughter, 11 year-old Mary, was bound out shortly
after. His three sons—William, Barney, and John—left the Almshouse
with him in May 1825, but returned the following month without him.
Previous Stint: January 2, 1824 to May 28, 1825 (discharged with father)

BARNEY CARROLL, 6
Birth: 1819, Baltimore
Admitted: June 7, 1825   Exit: discharged with brother John,
                                August 15, 1825
Malady: deserted by his father
Previous Stint: January 2, 1824 to May 28, 1825 (discharged with father)

JOHN CARROLL, 4
Birth: 1821, Baltimore
Admitted: June 7, 1825   Exit: discharged with brother Barney,
                                 August 15, 1825
Malady: deserted by his father
Previous Stint: January 2, 1824 to May 28, 1825 (discharged with father)

MARGARET (PEGGY) MARRS, 40
Birth: 1785
Admitted: June 7, 1825   Exit: died in the Almshouse
                                 January 16, 1826
Previous Stints: May 2, 1823 to June 18, 1823 (ran-away); September 26,
1823 to October 21, 1823 (eloped[1]); October 24, 1823 to December 26,
1823 (eloped); January 6, 1824 to May 30, 1825 (eloped)

MARGARET SOUGLE, 69
Birth: 1756, Ireland   Religion: Catholic
Admitted: June 7, 1825   Exit: discharged March 28, 1826
Malady: old age

WILLIAM ACKERMAN, 23
Birth: 1802, Baltimore
Occupation: blacksmith   Religion: Lutheran
Admitted: June 8, 1825   Exit: eloped June 15, 1825
Malady: deranged by drink   Other: uses tobacco

HUGH GERVIN, 83
Birth: 1742, Ireland
Residence: lived in Baltimore since 1823; in the U.S. since 1785
Religion: Presbyterian
Admitted: June 8, 1825   Exit: discharged August 1, 1825
Malady: old age and spitting blood

PHILIP HARMAN, 63
Birth: 1762, Pennsylvania
Residence: lived in Baltimore since 1785
Occupation: carpenter   Religion: Lutheran

---

[1] *eloped:* ran away without performing enough labor to clear one's debts for room and board.

Admitted: June 8, 1825   Exit: discharged March 28, 1826
Other: uses tobacco

SAMUEL MONTGOMERY, 49
Birth: 1776, Ireland
Residence: lived in U.S. since 1803; in Baltimore 1 day
Occupation: shoemaker   Religion: Presbyterian
Admitted: June 8, 1825   Exit: discharged July 2, 1825
Malady: had been in the Philadelphia Almshouse
                         Other: uses tobacco

DONALD MCDONALD, 103
Birth: 1722, Ireland
Residence: lived in U.S. since 1752; in Baltimore 1 day
Occupation: labourer   Religion: Catholic
Admitted: June 11, 1825   Exit: eloped July 5, 1825
Malady: a runaway from the Philadelphia Almshouse
                         Other: uses tobacco

WILLIAM H. BUEL, 54
Birth: 1771, New York
Residence: lived in Baltimore since 1797
Occupation: mariner   Religion: none
Admitted: June 12, 1825   Exit: eloped June 20, 1825
Malady: diarhoea from drunkenness
                         Other: uses tobacco

ANN [NANCY] PETERS, 50
Birth: 1775, Baltimore County
Residence: lived in Baltimore since 1805
Religion: Presbyterian
Admitted: June 12, 1825   Exit: died in the Almshouse
                         August 26, 1825

Malady: lame arm and sore
Previous Stint: in the Almshouse in 1820; May 18, 1824 to March 1, 1825
(discharged)

JANE MCCAULLAY, 21
Birth: 1804, Ireland
Residence: in the U.S. 1 month; in Baltimore 1 day
Religion: Protestant Episcopalian

Admitted: June 13, 1825   Exit: discharged July 6, 1825
Malady: pregnant, says she was shipwrecked and lost her husband and child

JAMES WILSON, 44
Birth: 1781, Baltimore
Occupation: carpenter   Religion: none
Admitted: June 14, 1825   Exit: discharged, March 4, 1826
Malady: drunk when admitted, sprained wrist

ELIZABETH YOUNG, 17, coloured[2]
Birth: 1808, Washington
Residence: lived in Baltimore since 1821
Occupation: housework   Religion: none
Admitted: June 14, 1825   Exit: eloped September 15, 1825
Malady: venereal

RICHARD EAGEN, 59
Birth: 1766, Baltimore
Occupation: carpenter   Religion: Baptist
Admitted: June 17, 1825   Exit: discharged December 16, 1825
Malady: ulcer on the leg
Other: would return to Almshouse for 1 month in 1826 with venereal condition and ulcer on the leg

AMEY BULL, 53, Negro
Birth: 1772
Admitted: June 18, 1825   Exit: died in the Almshouse
                             October 4, 1826
Malady: brought from jail—insane
Previous Stint: April 29, 1823 to July 28, 1823 (eloped)

NANCY CHASE, 50, coloured
Birth: 1775, Harford County, Maryland
Admitted: June 18, 1825   Exit: eloped March 8, 1826
Malady: insane—brought from jail

---

[2]The clerk listed African American inmates as "coloured," "Negro," "Black," and "mulatto." Although the last term indicates someone having a "white" parent, the different connotations of the first three terms are not clear.

WILLIAM GILBREATH, 27
Birth: 1798, Baltimore
Admitted: June 18, 1825   Exit: eloped July 30, 1825
Malady: insane
Previous Stints: June 24, 1823 to August 12, 1823 (eloped); November 18, 1824 to February 25, 1825 (eloped)—in both cases sent to Almshouse from jail.
Other: would return to the Almshouse as a vagrant, November 29, 1825 to March 23, 1826 (eloped)

THOMAS STALLINGS, 25
Birth: 1800, Maryland
Residence: in Baltimore 3 months, previously in Philadelphia
Occupation: blockmaker   Religion: Methodist
Admitted: June 18, 1825   Exit: eloped August 7, 1825
Malady: venereal   Other: uses tobacco

JAMES CONNER [CONNELL], 64
Birth: 1761, Ireland
Residence: lived in Baltimore since 1784
Occupation: baker   Religion: Catholic
Admitted: June 21, 1825   Exit: discharged August 30, 1825
Malady: rheumatism
Other: uses tobacco; would return to Almshouse from November 3, 1825 to May 23, 1826

CATHERINE FOSS, 35
Birth: 1790, Massachusetts
Residence: lived in Baltimore since 1815
Religion: Methodist
Admitted: June 22, 1825   Exit: died in the Almshouse
                                               August 27, 1825
Malady: dropsey
Other: arrived at the Almshouse with 2 sons [see below]; a third child reported to be hers arrived at the Almshouse in October and was bound out soon after.

JOHN FOSS, 8
Birth: August 6, 1816, Baltimore
Admitted: June 22, 1825   Exit: bound out as apprentice
                                               July 18, 1825

WILLIAM HENRY FOSS, 6
Birth: August 10, 1818, Baltimore
Admitted: June 22, 1825   Exit: bound out as apprentice
                                 September 26, 1825

MARY GORE, 44
Birth: 1781, Virginia
Residence: lived in Baltimore since 1799
Occupation: spin, card, knit, &c.
                                 Religion: Catholic
Admitted: June 22, 1825   Exit: discharged June 7, 1826
Malady: rheumatism   Other: uses tobacco

ZACHARIAH STALLINS, 30
Birth: 1795, Calvert County, Maryland
Residence: lived in Baltimore since 1799
Occupation: labourer   Religion: none
Admitted: June 22, 1825   Exit: eloped July 30, 1825
Malady: venereal
Other: uses tobacco; would return with daughter (Elizabeth, 9) to Alms-
house for two months in January 1826[3]

SALSBURY WILEY, 47
Birth: 1778
Religion: Presbyterian
Admitted: June 22, 1825   Exit: discharged October 3, 1825
Malady: nearly blind
Previous Stints: January 9, 1819 to April 19, 1819; March 5, 1823 to
February 1, 1825; February 12, 1825 to March 29, 1825 (discharged
all three times).
Other: would return to Almshouse due to want of employment, Novem-
ber 12, 1825 to March 12, 1826 (discharged)

---

[3]Zachariah Stallins stirred up a controversy in early 1827 when he attempted to reen-
ter the almshouse, having eloped several times before. When the overseer, Mr. Morton,
turned Stallins away, the rebuffed pauper asked, "Am I to die in the street?" Because
Morton supposedly nodded in assent, the manager of the poor from Stallins's neighborhood threatened to resign. In his defense, Morton explained: "I am at least *certain* that I
never gave such an answer to any person whom I thought in danger of a fate so dreadful *in consequence of that answer;* but if a sturdy vagrant, or one labouring under no dis-
ability but what a few hours of abstinence from liquor would remove . . . had asked me
whether he was to perish in the street, it is possible, that I might have replied in the
affirmative to the hypocritical query."

JOSEPH BRUCE, 42
Birth: 1783, England
Residence: lived in Baltimore since 1817
Occupation: weaver   Religion: none
Admitted: June 23, 1825   Exit: died in the Almshouse
                              June 24, 1825
Malady: intemperance and bruises

MATILDA GRAY, 30
Birth: 1795, Maryland
Residence: lived in Baltimore since 1811
Occupation: spin, knit, & housework
                              Religion: Methodist
Admitted: June 23, 1825   Exit: discharged October 3, 1825
Malady: rheumatism   Other: uses tobacco

JOHN RILEY (the 2nd), 34
Birth: 1791, Ireland
Residence: lived in Baltimore since 1806
Occupation: painter   Religion: Presbyterian
Admitted: June 23, 1825   Exit: discharged October 3, 1825
Malady: swollen feet   Other: uses tobacco

ADAM THOMPSON, 62
Birth: 1763, Ireland
Occupation: no trade   Religion: Presbyterian
Admitted: June 23, 1825   Exit: died in the Almshouse
                              May 30, 1826
Malady: one-legged; drunkenness
                              Other: uses tobacco, can read and write
Previous Stints: May 26, 1823 to October 28, 1823 (eloped); November 7, 1823 (suicidal when admitted) to April 26, 1825 (discharged)

ELIZABETH RELAND, newborn
Birth: June 24, 1825 in the Almshouse to Mary Ann Reland, a 21 year-old German Lutheran who had arrived to Baltimore in 1819 and entered the Almshouse on April 18, 1825, pregnant.
Exit: discharged with mother July 9, 1825
Other: father is Frederick Hess—Butcher who formerly lived with Mr. Cry on Federal Hill

DANIEL M. CASEY, 57
Birth: 1768, Calvert County, Maryland
Residence: in Baltimore 1 day, last in Georgetown, District of Columbia
Religion: Methodist
Admitted: June 25, 1825   Exit: died in the Almshouse
                              July 4, 1826
Malady: colic   Other: uses tobacco

JOSEPH COLLINS, 33
Birth: 1792, Maryland
Residence: lived in Baltimore since 1795
Occupation: sailor   Religion: Catholic
Admitted: June 25, 1825   Exit: discharged—and taken by the
                              Sheriff on a charge of felony
                              July 1, 1825
Malady: drunkenness and sore leg
                              Other: uses tobacco
Previous Stint: February 20, 1823 to November 23, 1824 (discharged)

SAMUEL McELROY, 56
Birth: 1769, Philadelphia
Residence: lived in Baltimore since 1816
Occupation: cabinet maker   Religion: Presbyterian
Admitted: June 25, 1825   Exit: died in the Almshouse
                              August 17, 1825
Malady: crazy from drink   Other: uses tobacco
Previous Stint: August 7, 1824 to August 31, 1824 (eloped)

JOHN WATSON, 50
Birth: 1775, Ireland
Residence: lived in Baltimore since 1802
Occupation: labourer   Religion: Episcopalian
Admitted: June 25, 1825   Exit: discharged August 24, 1825
Malady: injured by the fall of a house

JOHN COCHRAN, 46
Birth: 1779, Ireland
Residence: lived in Baltimore since 1816
Occupation: sailor   Religion: Catholic
Admitted: June 26, 1825   Exit: discharged October 11, 1825
Malady: consumption   Other: uses tobacco

DAVID RIGGIN, 52
Birth: 1773, Maryland
Residence: lived in Baltimore since 1801
Occupation: carpenter   Religion: Episcopalian
Admitted: June 27, 1825   Exit: discharged February 13, 1826
Malady: intemperance
Previous Stints: May 23, 1825 to June 23, 1825 (eloped)
Other: uses tobacco; would return to the Almshouse, February 16, 1826
to March 13, 1826 (eloped)

ELIZABETH DAVIS, 22
Birth: 1803, Eastern Shore, Maryland
Residence: lived in Baltimore since 1820
Occupation: spin, card, knit, weave
                              Religion: none
Admitted: June 29, 1825   Exit: eloped August 2, 1825
Malady: venereal   Other: uses tobacco

CARILINE CORNISH, 14, Black
Birth: 1811, Philadelphia
Residence: lived in Baltimore since 1823
Occupation: housework
Admitted: June 30, 1825   Exit: eloped September 11, 1825
Malady: venereal   Other: uses tobacco

17

Report of the Trustees
of the Baltimore Almshouse

1827

This report covers the men and women admitted to the Baltimore almshouse in June 1825. Compare the trustees' findings with the raw data in Document 16. Each year, the almshouse trustees compiled statistics from the admissions book and reported to the mayor and city council.

Report of the Trustees of the Alms-House for Baltimore City and County—1827, Baltimore City Archives.

They touted their successes in keeping expenses low, in extracting productive labor from inmates, and in curing them of diseases. Their annual operating budget for the previous year had been just over $19,000, which included $2,200 to maintain 137 pensioners in their own homes. Compared to the poor-relief budgets of other large cities, Baltimore's expenses were minimal (see Document 18). Baltimore's almshouse kept expenses low by relying on the labor of its inhabitants to raise crops, sew clothing, and maintain the facilities. Indeed, in the period covered by this report, pauper labor produced 3,710 square yards of fabric, 666 pairs of shoes, 53 barrels of soap, 369 coffins, 16,020 heads of cabbage, and 1,735 pounds of butter. Still, the trustees warned, greater efforts were necessary to keep people out of the almshouse in the first place. Consider how the tables included with this report allowed the trustees to draw conclusions about the causes and character of urban poverty.

. . . It is with much satisfaction that the Trustees are enabled to state to the Mayor and City Council, that the same excellent discipline good order and economy which have for several years past distinguished the Alms House, continue to be maintained there; and that the school for the education of the children, has been regularly kept; the average number taught being between 40 and 50, and also that religious service is regularly performed in the House at least once a week, at which times the Paupers, whose state of health will admit of it, very generally attend.

The Alms House at Calverton, under its present organization embraces several objects, which are naturally connected with the Institution, and which it is believed greatly extend the value of the establishment.

First.—It contains an Infirmary for the indigent sick.

Secondly.—A Lying-in Hospital.[1]

Thirdly.—A Work House for the employment of vagrants, and such of the poor as may be capable of contributing in some degree, towards their own support.

Fourthly.—An asylum for destitute children, in which upwards of one hundred are generally supported, and an average of about half that number receive the benefit of school education.

Fifthly.—A Lunatic Hospital, and

Sixthly.—Upon the foregoing Establishments there is engrafted a medical and chirurgical[2] school, in which a highly advantageous

[1] *Lying-in hospital:* maternity ward.
[2] *chirurgical:* surgical.

opportunity is afforded, for the advancement and diffusion of knowledge in these important branches of science.

. . . [I]t will be seen that the actual cost to the City for supporting each pauper in the year 1822 was $44 17 cts. and that this cost has been gradually reduced until in the year ending with April, 1826, the period at which this Report closes, it was only $37 63 cts. for each pauper per annum. . . . This abatement in the expenses the Trustees believe arises partly from the reduction in the cost of the articles of food and clothing furnished to the House; but principally from the introduction of a more rigid system of economy into the establishment, and the increased value of the labour performed by such of the vagrants and paupers there, as are capable of contributing in some degree towards their own support.

. . . [I]t will be seen that the value of the articles raised and furnished on the farm the present year is estimated at $3,971, and that the value of the labour performed and of the articles manufactured in the House is $3,194, which two items constitute an available resource, towards the support of the establishment, of more than ($7000,) Seven Thousand Dollars, whilst under the system of cultivation now pursued on the farm, the soil is fast improving, and its productiveness will become hereafter greatly increased.

When it is recollected that of the persons usually in the Alms House, about one hundred are children, more than one hundred are sick, nearly a hundred consist of infirm and maimed persons incapable of labour, and that of those remaining more than half are necessarily employed in the duties of attending upon the three first recited classes, or of keeping the House and premises clean and in good order, and when it is also considered that the remainder is mostly composed of persons of enfeebled constitutions, and of indolent habits, it will be admitted that the effective labour drawn from them, as exhibited in the document here referred to, both as regards the quantity and value of the articles produced, is as much as under such circumstances could reasonably be expected.

In a country where the means of obtaining a comfortable subsistence are so abundant as in this community, and where labour is at the same time so amply rewarded, and so wholly unincumbered by taxation or any kind of burthen, it must naturally excite astonishment, that there should be found so large a mass of poverty as is concentrated in the Alms House of Baltimore City and County, and when we consider that this mass is constantly augmenting, both in magnitude and depravity, it surely becomes a matter of serious importance to investigate the causes which have led, and are still leading, to this melancholy exhibit of human suffering and demoralization.

The Trustees deeply impressed with the responsibility which from their situation necessarily devolves upon them, have thought it their duty to take measures to enquire into these causes, and they now lay before the Mayor and City Council the result of their investigation.... By this it appears that of the 623 adult persons admitted into the Alms House during the year ending April, 1826, FIVE HUNDRED AND FIFTY FOUR were positively ascertained to have been reduced to the necessity of being placed there by drunkenness, and it is believed that a considerable portion of the remaining 69, were likewise reduced to the same necessity, either remotely or directly by the same cause; in addition to which it should be further remarked, that of the great number of children who are always in the House, there is scarce an instance occurs of one being placed there, who has not been reduced to that necessity, by the intemperance either of one or both of its parents.

Monthly Entrance and Exit Figures

	Admitted.	Born.	Total.	Discharged.	Bound.	Died.	Eloped.	Total.
1825.			INGRESS.					EGRESS.
May	47		47	43	7	12	14	76
June	51	3	54	30	3	9	19	61
July	47	1	48	28	3	12	18	61
August	65	2	67	24		16	10	50
September	63		63	19	1	16	18	54
October	64		64	20	5	17	7	49
November	68	3	71	12	2	23	11	48
December	76	1	77	15	5	17	17	54
January, 1826 ..	70	1	71	20	2	18	6	46
February	60	2	62	15	1	14	17	47
March	46	2	48	60	2	14	20	96
April	65	2	67	32	2	17	17	68
	722	17	739	318	33	185	174	710

In the House, April 30th, 1825, ... .386

Total Ingress, ... .739

1,125

Total Egress, ... .710

In the House, April 30th, 1826, ... .415

That an evil of so gigantic and overwhelming magnitude should so long have been permitted to extend its destructive ravages, without calling forth the united efforts of the moral part of the community, to restrain or counteract its progress, is indeed matter of equal regret and astonishment, and the Trustees in now inviting the consideration of the constituted authorities of the City to this momentous subject, would earnestly hope that it may receive that grave and serious attention to which its vast importance gives it a claim. . . .

Monthly Census

1825.	WHITE.			COLOURED.				WHERE FROM.			
	Men.	Women.	Children.	Men.	Women.	Children.	Total.	City.	County.	Elsewhere.	Total.
May.	109	116	62	21	34	15	357	301	34	22	357
June.	111	119	60	18	30	12	350	291	34	25	350
July.	107	110	64	17	29	10	337	278	34	25	337
August.	110	111	70	20	29	14	354	286	40	28	354
September.	116	113	74	21	30	9	363	304	35	24	363
October.	125	115	72	24	33	9	378	311	38	29	378
November.	132	125	74	21	33	16	401	319	45	37	401
December.	133	140	79	21	38	13	424	341	44	39	424
January, 1826. . .	137	141	90	24	47	10	449	372	39	38	449
February.	138	154	90	29	46	7	464	388	43	33	464
March.	118	134	84	27	44	9	416	337	45	34	416
April.	116	135	83	25	45	11	415	340	41	34	415
	1452	1513	902	268	438	1135	4708	3868	472	368	4708

Statement of the Number of Persons received into the Alms-House of the City and County of Baltimore, from the 1st of May, 1825, to the 30th of April, 1826, inclusive, exhibiting their places of Birth, Diseases, and the Causes, as far as the same have been ascertained, which led to their admission.

Baltimore City,	147
Baltimore County,	66
Eastern Shore of Maryland,	100
Other parts of Maryland,	69
Pennsylvania,	40
Virginia,	19
Other parts of the United States,	47
England,	31
Ireland,	156
Scotland,	8
Germany,	24
Holland,	6
Other parts of Europe,	8
West Indies,	7
Unknown,	11
Whole number received,	739

Debility from intemperance,	235	
Maniac from drunkenness,	54	
Venereal, every individual of these being addicted to intemperance,	85	
Ulcers, the effect of drunkenness,	34	
Fractures and Wounds which in every case were received whilst the parties were in a state of intoxication,	28	
Various diseases, all traced to drunkenness,	104	
Crippled whilst the parties were in a state of intoxication,	7	
Old age, all habitual drunkards	7	
		554
Pregnancy,	19	
Various diseases, the causes not known,	10	
Crippled from accidents,	6	
Insanity,	11	
Old Age, the habits of the parties unknown,	5	
Decayed health, the habits of the parties not known,	15	
		69
Children,		116
Total number received, as above stated,		739

18

Philadelphia Board
of Guardians of the Poor
1827

The instinct to study poverty led poor-relief administrators to send delegations to other cities to gather ideas for reducing expenses and improving administrative practices. The four Philadelphians who traveled to Baltimore, New York, Providence, Boston, and Salem in 1827 received a rude shock: Every other city had a better system. Philadelphia's total expenses dwarfed those of New York, a city that contained an additional 50,000 inhabitants. No other city offered outdoor relief as abundantly as Philadelphia, and as a result, no other city appeared to have Philadelphia's mass of able-bodied paupers and unwed mothers. The committee returned to Philadelphia and penned a report that ultimately led to an overhaul of the city's relief program the following year. "The time has arrived to commence, if not fully to accomplish a radical reform," they declared. As recommended, outdoor aid would be stopped, and anyone desiring relief would have to submit to the discipline of the almshouse.

... On a careful consideration of what has been stated, your committee cannot but admit the mortifying fact, that every system they have examined is superior to our own. ...

... That we have been prosecuting a career of error, is sufficiently obvious, and the natural consequence is a co-extensive increase of misery and profligacy, of idleness and crime. The incentives to industry have been weakened, the ties which connect society relaxed, and the desire of honest independence lessened, among that class of the community, to whom honesty, industry and sobriety are peculiarly indispensable. For take from the man, whose lot it is to labour day by day for his daily bread, these essential qualifications, and suffer him to become the degraded recipient of public charity, without having been compelled to it by sorrow and suffering, arising from causes beyond his control, and if he ever again emerge from degradation, or elevate

---

Report of the Committee Appointed by the Board of Guardians of the Poor of the City and Districts of Philadelphia, to Visit the Cities of Baltimore, New-York, Providence, Boston, and Salem (Philadelphia: Samuel Parker, 1827), 23–30.

himself to respectability, he must possess redeeming qualities, that rarely fall to the lot of his fellow man.

Your committee can with confidence assert, that the experience of all places, where the system of out-door relief has prevailed, leads to the same conclusion, namely, *"That of all modes of providing for the Poor, the most wasteful, the most expensive, and the most injurious to their morals, and destructive of their industrious habits, is that of supply in their own families."* Ample illustrations might be adduced, to show the justice of this opinion. "The manner in which public charity is too often administered," (says the report from the Beverly Poor-house) "affords encouragement to idleness, intemperance, and improvidence. The idle will beg, in preference to working: relief is extended to them without suitable discrimination. They are not left to feel the just consequences of their own idleness. The industrious poor are discouraged, by observing that bounty bestowed upon the idle, which they can only obtain by the sweat of their brow. Our climate indicates the necessity of forecast. If in summer the poor expend all the produce of their labour, in winter they will be in want. This improvidence may be, and often is encouraged, by the facility with which relief is obtained under pressing circumstances. At the time they are misspending or wasting their earnings, if they reflect at all, it will be that when winter comes upon them, and they are cut off from labour, they have a resource in the charity of individuals, and if not, they can obtain relief by application to the overseers of the poor."

If out-door relief be given at all, the manner of administering it adopted by the town of Salem, is the least objectionable of any that has come under our notice: viz. in donations of wood and provisions, distributed at the Alms House, by the steward, under the direction of the overseers; *and no money in any case to be given.* But even this mode is liable to great abuse; and indeed, what plan could be adopted, which trick and imposture and indolence, would not continually overreach? In short, the whole system is essentially founded in error, and all its parts are consequently defective.

It is an axiom abundantly confirmed by experience, that in proportion to the means of support, provided for the poor and improvident, they are found to increase and multiply. This is a fact that should be kept in view by the directors of every Poor corporation; and they should remember, that they are not appointed and invested with power, for the purpose of giving encouragement to intemperance and vice, by affording desirable asylums for their unprincipled votaries. . . .

The poor in consequence of vice, constitute here and every where, by far the greater part of the poor. The experience of every Institution your committee has visited is decisive on this point. From three-fourths to nine-tenths of the paupers in all parts of our country, may attribute their degradation to the vice of intemperance. Whether the passage of a law similar to that of Baltimore, which compels the inmates of their Alms House, to remain, until they have performed a sufficiency of labour to repay their expenses, would here be expedient, is a question we leave for the consideration of the Board. Two preceding Boards have answered it in the affirmative.

The Trustees of the Baltimore establishment, are unanimously of opinion, that this regulation is decidedly beneficial, and thus far has exceeded their most sanguine expectation. It is the most important feature of their whole system; and its operation enables them to effect several desirable ends, of hitherto very difficult accomplishment. In the first place, it empowers them to derive an income from that class who are always the greatest burthen, namely, the intemperate, and at the same time rids them entirely of the charge of numbers. It also enables them to turn to some account, another description of unworthy poor, whose relief is extremely onerous; viz. syphilitic cases, particularly female. To these, our Alms House is a resource for maintenance during the continuance of disease, contracted solely by their own vices. When cured, they demand their discharge, and immediately return to their former courses, and are in a short time again applicants for relief, and always at a more than proportionate expense, as they are under medical treatment during the whole period of their stay. Many of these, even when attacked with disease, would be extremely cautious of applying for admission on such terms; and by finding that impunity did not always follow their irregularities, might haply acquire sufficient forecast to avoid them for the future. . . .

The practice of the Trustees of Baltimore, since the introduction of their new system, is a sufficient illustration of these sentiments. The diminution of the out-door relief, and the methodical employment exacted within, have been attended with such encouraging success, and have so greatly lessened the number of paupers, as to leave no doubt of the propriety of their plans, nor uncertainty with regard to their ultimate accomplishment.

One of the greatest burthens that falls upon this corporation, is the maintenance of the host of worthless foreigners, disgorged upon our shores. The proportion is so large, and so continually increasing, that we are imperatively called upon to take some steps to arrest its progress. It is neither reasonable nor just, nor politic, that we should incur so heavy an expense in the support of people, who never have, *nor never will* contribute one cent to the benefit of this community, and who have in many instances been public paupers in their own country. If ever the trite adage, "that charity begins at home," be adopted as a rule of conduct, either by individuals or communities, it is especially under circumstances like the present, that it should be admitted in its fullest extent; and that the people of this district, should unresistingly suffer it to become the reservoir into which Europe may pour her surplus of worthlessness, improvidence and crime, exhibits a degree of forbearance and recklessness altogether inexcusable.

The adoption of a regulation sanctioned by law, obliging all merchants and captains to furnish a list of the passengers they may import, immediately on arrival, and either to give security they shall not become a public charge, or to commute the cases by the payment of a certain sum per head, would in a degree remedy the evil. Such is the regulation at New-York, and ... the sum derived therefrom amounts to 10,000 dollars per annum; or if the legislature of our state would extend to us the same liberality evinced by the legislatures of New-York, Massachusetts and Connecticut, in annually appropriating a specific sum for the relief of cases of this kind, our burthen would be considerably lightened. The chances, however, of aid from this source are too small to be much calculated upon, or to excite very sanguine expectations. . . .

The usage of this Board with regard to cases of bastardy, is one of the most odious features in their whole system, inasmuch as it is an encouragement to vice, and offers a premium for prostitution. If such be the fact, it ill becomes an assemblage of married men, the fathers of families, to persist in vindicating either its propriety or its policy. Though your committee are not prepared to say, that it is the particular province or duty of the Board of guardians in their collective capacity, to recall the wanderer from the error of his ways, yet we may most assuredly assert, that they are bound to afford no inducements to a departure from virtue. And if the extending relief to all cases of this nature that come under their notice, if paying a regular stipend from the public purse, whenever the female cannot find a profitable father for her offspring, be not affording countenance and encouragement, then are your committee ignorant of the meaning of words, and incapable of estimating the moral consequences of things.

To show the miserable effects of our ill advised system on this head, we have only to contrast its results, with the practice adopted by our sister institutions in like cases, and it can no longer be regarded as problematical, that ours is wrong in all its features and bearings, and exhibits an anomaly altogether unique, and such [h]as excited the surprise of all persons in other places to whom it was described. Indeed they could hardly realize the existence of a state of things so contrary to their own practice, and so evidently tending to unnecessary expense, and unavoidable immorality. Thus in Baltimore, the trustees for the poor expressly stated, that they did not consider themselves subjected to any expense on this head; in New York 80 or 90 cases come under their notice; in Boston *nine or ten,* in Salem *two* or *three,* and in Philadelphia 269!!! a difference which can never be accounted for by greater population, nor by any alleged or supposed inferiority of moral feeling or principle. Does it not rather arise from the support and countenance held forth on the one hand, and the absolute denial of them on the other; from the impunity with which decorum and virtue are set at nought within our borders, and the restraint, reproof, and punishment, which elsewhere attend their violation? Let any one whose convictions on this point are not sufficiently clear, attend at this room on the day when the committee on bastardy pay the weekly allowances to their pensioners, and mark the unblushing effrontery, that some of them exhibit. The thanklessness with which they receive their allotted stipend; the insolence with which they demand a further supply, arrogantly exacting as a *right,* what ought never to have been granted, even as a charity....

It is time to bring these observations to a close; they are extended to a greater length than was anticipated by your committee on commencing them. They will only remark in conclusion, that while admitting the inferiority of our own institutions, compared with those they have visited, they find consolation in the reflection, that as the cause of this inferiority is sufficiently obvious, the means of improvement are abundantly within our reach....

Structural Explanations
and Cures for Poverty

19

Petition of New Jersey Working Widows to the U.S. Senate

1816

Supporters of American textile manufacturing saw an untapped resource in the labor of the urban poor, especially females. To this end, the Pennsylvania Society for the Encouragement of Manufactures and the Useful Arts was founded in 1787. More famously, Alexander Hamilton and his associates opened a manufacturing village in Paterson, New Jersey, in 1792. By the early 1810s, a significant number of poor women had left cities to labor in manufacturing villages that dotted the countryside. Work was abundant during the years of conflict with Great Britain, but the end of the War of 1812 allowed cheap English imports to flood American markets. Textile villages ceased production, and many working families lost the means of support. This remarkable petition resulted in the passage of a protective tariff in 1816 to exclude foreign cotton textiles. Such tariffs would remain in place through the 1820s but did not guarantee a subsistence to working families.

U.S. Senate, 14th Congress, 1st Session, National Archives, Legislative Reference Section, RG 46, Sen 14A-C6. Reprinted in Alfred D. Chandler, *The New American State Papers: Manufactures* (Wilmington, Del.: Scholarly Resources, 1972), 1:439.

14th Congress, 1st Session   U.S. Senate

Petition of a number of widows, orphans and families of New Manchester N.J. in behalf of domestic manufacturing

FEBRUARY 5, 1816

TO THE HONORABLE THE SENATE AND HOUSE OF REPRESENTATIVES OF THE UNITED STATES IN CONGRESS ASSEMBLED.

THE PETITION OF THE WIDOWS AND ORPHANS AND FAMILYS OF THE TOWN OF NEW MANCHESTER, COUNTY BERGEN HUMBLY SHEWETH

That your Petitioners from the demand for labor of Persons in the various branches of the Cotton Manufactures were led to settle with their families in this Town, and previously to the peace were enabled by the strictest Economy to support, some of them their infirm Parents and some of them their fatherless Infants; with some degree of decency and Comfort, your Petitioners have found themselves at a subsequent period altho plunged into Difficulties, still enabled to obtain some of the necessaries of Life yet struggling with embarrassments too numerous to trouble your honorable body with the recital of.

They struggled however, cheered by hope and with resignation waited for better times; fallacious has been our expectations, and the latter Crisis has brought us of that Hope the only remaining Comfort of the wretched. Dispair now stares up on us with horrid Aspect and we view no other prospect but that of absolute Nakedness. The severity of the present Season adds to our other distress, our helpless Infants crying for bread to those to whom support is withheld crying with pitious Accents, with the pains of frozen limbs and Disease incident to poverty of our Situation, some of those indeed for whom they toiled now snatched to that world where they shall hunger no more and no more be witness to the miseries of their helpless families altho it might relive the accumulated purpose of their wants, adds ten fold misery to the finer feelings of their Souls, your Petitioners approach your honorable body emboldened yet respectfully by the urgency of their situation to pray your honorable body to view with commiseration their distress and extend aid to them by granting such encouragement to the Cotton Manufacturing Establishments which you may deem conducive to the general Interests of our Country and for which your petitioners with tens of thousands of distressed females as in duty bound will ever pray.

New Manchester Bergen Co.   New Jersey 18 January 1816

20

The Working People
of New Castle County, Delaware
1829

As their prospects for upward mobility narrowed at the end of the 1820s, skilled artisans (especially those at the journeyman level) developed a stinging critique of American inequality. Wrapping themselves in the republican ideology of the American Revolution, militant workers formed new organizations in large cities like New York and Philadelphia, as well as in small communities like New Castle County, Delaware. These unions and workingmen's parties shared a belief that laboring people could use the strength of numbers to protect their interests. If government could be put into the service of the many instead of the few, it would be possible to fulfill the destiny of the Revolution. On a more mundane level, it would be possible for working men and women to stave off poverty.

FELLOW CITIZENS AND FELLOW LABORERS,

The Association of Working People having at length become organised, have deemed it expedient to address you, with a view of making known to you their intentions and at the same time engaging your assistance in carrying their views into effect.

The Working People have been emphatically denominated the "bone and sinew" of the body politic; and this is true, inasmuch as they are the most numerous and at the same time the most useful of all classes in which men are divided; it being by them that all things are made, that are made for the use of man, by the power of art in peace; and they forming in war their country's principal and sure defence; while to say the least, *some* of the other classes are mere drones in the hive, who not only live upon the product of the working man's labor, but in fact, appropriate a much larger share to themselves, than the producer himself is able to enjoy.

And, Fellow Citizens, why are these things so? Why is it that one class of men are sunk so far below the rest, in a country which has declared to the universe, that "all men are created free and equal?" Have we not laws to secure to us that "Freedom and Equality" to

Free Enquirer, October 7, 1829.

obtain which our forefathers opposed the legions of Britain in the dark days of the Revolution? No! the poor have no laws; the laws are made by the rich, and of course *for* the rich.

It is a lamentable fact, that though we are nominally a "governing and self governed people," still there are a privileged few who lord it over us as though we were not fit to claim an equality with them, treating us as though we were made of different and less costly materials than they, even while we have been the means of their advancement; making us, as it were, the ladder by which they climb into office; and when they have arrived at the desired height, kicking the ladder down.

The question that naturally arises is, how are these things to be remedied? We answer by *union among the working people.* Too long have we slumbered! and "remember that it was while sleeping that Sampson was shorn of his locks." Too long have ye been the willing dupes of the demon, party spirit; too long have ye neglected your own interest and suffered yourselves to be led away by the "magic of a name;" giving your suffrages to men who have looked down from the height to which YOU exalted them, with the most sovereign contempt for your blindness to your own interests.

Arise then in your strength, and when called upon to exercise the distinctive privilege of a *freeman,* the "elective franchise," give your votes to no man who is not pledged to support your interests. You will ask where are we to find such men? Are not the interests of the non-producing classes in direct opposition to the interests of the laborer? and is it not in the ranks of these classes, that we are accustomed to find men best qualified for the office of Legislators, as but few of our own class have received the benefits of a liberal education?

We can but answer, True: and pity that it is true. But at the same time we ask again, why are these things so? Is it not because the funds that should have been appropriated to a rational system of general education at the expense of the state, have been shamefully squandered and misapplied, and instead of being expended in the use of true Internal Improvement, in the improvement of the minds of the rising generation, they have been lavished for purposes of minor importance, while what little has been done towards a system of General Education, has been handed out as the dole of charity, and as such has been refused by all who though poor in worldly goods, are rich in an *independent republican spirit* which scorns to receive as a favor what it should demand as a right.

Let us then, Fellow Citizens, shake off the torpor of sloth and inactivity which has so long held us in ignominious thraldom; let every man come forward and use his utmost exertions to produce a system of instruction where the children of the rich and the poor shall be placed upon a level, and shall receive a National Education calculated to make *republicans* and banish *aristocrats,* which will never be the case, while our State Legislatures erect and endow Seminaries, Colleges and Academies, for the rich, and dole out charity schools for the poor.

Fellow citizens, let every man remember whatever may be his lot in life, whether of high or low degree, that he is an American, and a citizen of the United States; let him remember the awful responsibility which rests upon him in making a proper use of the invaluable privilege he possesses in the "elective franchise;" that it is not for himself alone that he acts, but for posterity; that, if it be too late to secure the blessings of education for himself, it is time he was up and doing to secure them for his children; thus to hasten the time when it cannot be said that want of education prevents the laboring classes from watching over their own interests.

We are pleased to find that a spirit of enquiry is abroad among our fellow workmen, which cannot but lead to the most beneficial results, as we are well aware that nothing is wanting but a knowledge of our rights to make all zealous in supporting them.

It is an established axiom that "knowledge is power;" and every day's experience, more forcibly impresses the truth of it upon our minds. There is no reason why knowledge should not be distributed among the poor as well as the rich. The working classes have been too long neglected and it is a disgrace to all Legislators from 1776, to the present day, that in this "enlightened age," as it is called, so many free born citizens of our happy country have been compelled by poverty to grovel in the darkness of ignorance, in many cases uncheered even by the faint glimmer of a Charity or Free School, as they are commonly called.

Ignorance and superstition go hand in hand: The mind once shackled, it is no difficult matter to enslave the body. And is there a man who will hesitate to come forward and use all his exertions, unite all his energies, to arrest (ere it be too late) so terrible an evil from our common country?

We hope to find that all will come forward and join in defence of their inalienable rights, lest these United States follow in the footsteps of Europe, and we find ourselves in the situation of the operatives of Great Britain, who are even now on the brink of starvation, from the effects of "labor saving machinery," while the non-producers, from the same cause, are rolling in wealth wrung from the labor of the despised operative.

Now! then, is the accepted time, and now is the day of your political salvation. Come forward with one accord, and show to the world, that you are in very deed what you profess to be, FREEMEN; and woe! to the traitor who would wish to brand you SLAVES.

21

THOMAS SKIDMORE

Rights of Man to Property
1829

Thomas Skidmore (1790–1832) presented an extensive plan for the elimination of property inheritance. Denying the sanctity of private property that stood at the center of Lockean political philosophy and the Anglo-American legal system, Skidmore invested government with the responsibility to keep property holding roughly equal by preventing the hereditary accumulation of wealth. As Skidmore explained, "Both rich and poor ought to be exterminated: the latter by being made what we may call rich; and the former by being brought to the common level." Under Skidmore's proposal, the property of everyone who died in a given year would revert back to the state, which in turn would distribute that property in equal shares to every male and female (white and black) who turned eighteen in that same year. In this excerpt, Skidmore identifies the equality of property as a natural right that the state must preserve.

. . . In order, therefore, to ascertain the poor man's rights, or the rich man's either, we must go back to the first formation of government. When we have done so; when we have ascended to the first era of society; where do we find our poor man? Where do we find our rich one? *They are no where to be seen.* Every thing is in common at this period. No man can call this tree his, or that the other's. No man can

Thomas Skidmore, *The Rights of Man to Property! Being a Proposition to Make It Equal among the Adults of the Present Generation* (New York: Alexander Ming Jr., 1829), 242–44, 283–84, 385–86.

say this field is mine; or that is yours. Field there is none. All is one wide common, unappropriate to any. How they *did* appropriate, when they resolved to divide among them, that which equally belonged to all, we may not know at present. But, how they *ought* to have divided, we know full well. It is engraved on the heart of man, and there is no power, while he lives and has his faculties, that can efface the engraving. That heart tells him, what it tells every man now who has one; that he has an equal right with any and every other man, to an equal share of the common property; or its undoubted equivalent. That heart tells him, that if, previous to any time, the soil, the common property of all has been pre-occupied by others, it is his right to demand an equivalent; or, as the only alternative left him, to enter by force, if necessary, into the possession of that which belongs equally to him, as to another. That heart tells every citizen of this State, or of any other State, that he, too, has the same inalienable right to his portion of the property of the State. That heart tells him, that if those who have first occupied this property, have done it in such a manner, *as to shut him out,* of his equal original right; and have not given him *his equivalent,* in lieu thereof, it is his *right,* and those who are in the same condition with him, to combine their exertions to produce such an arrangement, and division of the State, as will be able, even at this late, or at any later day, when they shall possess themselves of power enough to do so; to secure to themselves the enjoyment of their own equal portion. That heart tells him, that no length of time which oppression may have endured, can legalize its existence; and that the day of its death has come, when moral and physical power enough is found to exist to be able to destroy it.

How, then, if the present people of the State of New-York, had now for the first time, met on its soil, and were about to make appropriation of what they found here, how would they proceed? . . . Would they not divide the State as nearly equal as possible? Would they give to one man a territory, equal to the county of Rensselaer; to another a territory equal to the county of Putnam; and to a thousand, or ten thousand others, none at all, or any equivalent? Would the thousand or ten thousand, if they understood their rights, sanction such a division as this? Would they not overthrow it in an instant? And if, two hundred years ago, such an appropriation, or a similar one was made, shall it not be overthrown now? Shall it not be put out of existence now, and every thing, as it regards equality, be placed in the same condition as if it had never been? Is the error, is the injustice of such a distribution of the soil and property of the State, to receive our sanction because it has existed two centuries? . . .

... Thus far will it appear, that all governments may and ought to be put down, which do not preserve to all these rights. If it be *one* man's right, to let the earth out on hire, so is it another's; if one man may *not* sell to his fellow-men, the *use* of what God created for all, and for one as much as for another, so may not another. If one may live without labor, so may another; if one may live with *little* labor, so may another; if *one* must live by *much* labor, so must another; if one man may take another's labor, and appropriate it to the support of him who did not labor, so may any and every man do the same. If one may have, of the property of a generation, that has gone before us, five, or ten, or fifty, or a hundred, or five hundred thousand dollars; or a million, or five million, so may another, and every other. Nor is it to be said, even as things are now, that it is the dead who ever give property to their successors, after all. IT IS NOT THEY WHO GIVE: they have power to do nothing: for, if they had, many of them would carry it away with them to another world, if any such there be. It is THE LIVING who give the present holders of property the possession of it; *it is we ourselves,* (for in us and us alone, rests the title,) who have done it; and who yet allow it to be said, and hardly without a contradiction from us, that others have done it: it is a mistake: IT IS NONE BUT THE GENERATION PRESENT, — that gives, to what are called heirs, the possessions they enjoy; without this gift, this unjust and undeserved gift, they could not and would not have it at all! It is in OUR POWER, then, to CALL BACK the gift, whenever we shall think fit! That NOW IS THE TIME, need not further be shewn; for in showing that ALL MEN HAVE EQUAL RIGHTS, as well TO PROPERTY, as to life and liberty, every thing is shewn that is requisite. The time for *acting* on these principles is, when they are seen to be true; whenever they find a confirmation of their correctness in every human breast.

It remains then now, to speak more particularly of the methods which will be found most convenient in practice, to bring about the General Division in question. ...

... Take away from the possessors of the world their dividends, their rents, their profits; in one word, that which they receive for the *use* of it, and which belongs, freely belongs, to one as much as another; and what would become of the present miserable condition of the human race? It would be annihilated for ever. But these dividends, these rents, these profits, these prices paid for the *use* of the world, or of the world's materials, will never cease to be paid, till the *possession* of these materials is made equal, or substantially equal, among all men; till there shall be no lenders, no borrowers; no landlords, no tenants; no masters, no journeymen; no Wealth, no Want. ...

22

FRANCES WRIGHT

Lecture on Existing Evils and Their Remedy

1829

Frances Wright (1795–1852) earned her fame—or infamy—as one of the first women to deliver political speeches to male audiences. Born in Scotland, Wright first came to the United States in 1818 and returned again in 1825 to fight against slavery. Her critique of American society soon expanded to include organized religion, banking monopolies, and the subordination of women. Wright joined with Robert Dale Owen to edit the Free Enquirer, *a New York newspaper dedicated to free thought, birth control, and working-class politics. She and Owen advocated a national system of education in which the state would assume responsibility for raising and teaching every child under total equality. A new generation of republican children would instinctively eliminate the inequalities that marred American society. Wright and Owen faulted Skidmore's plan to redistribute property to adults, noting that without a comprehensive education system Skidmore's equality would be short-lived. But just as mainstream critics accused Skidmore of "agrarianism"—taking from the rich and giving to the poor—so too did they fault the national education plan for its reliance on extensive taxation of the rich to assist the poor.*

Who speaks of liberty while the human mind is in chains? Who of equality while the thousands are in squalid wretchedness, the millions harrassed with health destroying labor, the few afflicted with health-destroying idleness, and all tormented by health destroying solicitude? Look abroad on the misery which is gaining on the land! Mark the strife, and the discord, and the jealousies, the shock of interests and opinions, the hatreds of sect, the estrangements of class, the pride of wealth, the debasement of poverty, the helplessness of youth unprotected, of age uncomforted, of industry unrewarded, of ignorance unenlightened, of vice unreclaimed, of misery unpitied, of sickness, hunger, and nakedness unsatisfied, unalleviated, and unheeded. Go! mark all

The Free Enquirer, December 12, 1829.

the wrongs and the wretchedness with which the eye and the ear and the heart are familiar, and then echo in triumph and celebrate in jubilee the insulting declaration—*all men are free and equal!*

That evils exist, none that have eyes, ears and hearts can dispute. That these evils are on the increase, none who have watched the fluctuations of trade, the sinking price of labor, the growth of pauperism, and the increase of crime, will dispute. Little need be said here to the people of Philadelphia. The researches made by the public spirited among their own citizens, have but too well substantiated the suffering condition of a large mass of their population.[1] In Boston, in New York, in Baltimore, the voice of distress hath, in like manner, burst the barriers raised, and so long sustained, by the pride of honest industry, unused to ask from charity what it hath been wont to earn by the sweat of the brow. In each and every city necessity has constrained enquiry; and in each and every city enquiry has elicited the same appalling facts, that the hardest labor is often without a reward adequate to the sustenance of the laborer; that when, by overexertion and all the diseases, and often vices, which excess of exertion induces, the laborer, whose patient, sedulous industry supplies the community with all its comforts, and the rich with all their luxuries—when he, I say, is brought to an untimely grave by those exertions which, while sustaining the life of others, cut short his own—when he is mowed down by that labor whose products form the boasted wealth of the state, he leaves a family, to whom the strength of his manhood had barely furnished bread, to lean upon the weakness of a soul-stricken mother and hurry her to the grave of their father.

Such is the information gleaned from the report of the committee lately appointed by the town meeting of the city and county of Philadelphia, and as verbatim reiterated in every populous city throughout the land.[2] And what are the remedies suggested by our corporations, our newspaper editors, our religious societies, our tracts, and our sermons? Some have ordained facts, multiplied prayers, and re-recommended pious submission to a Providence who should have instituted all this calamity for the purpose of fulfilling the words of a Jewish prophet, "the poor shall never cease from the land."[3] Some, less-spiritual minded, have called for larger jails and more poor houses; some for increased

[1] Reports like Document 18.
[2] *Report of the Committee Appointed at a Town Meeting . . . to Consider the Subject of the Pauper System of the City and Districts, and to Report Remedies for Its Defects* (Philadelphia: Clark and Razer, 1827). This report was similar to Document 18.
[3] Deuteronomy 15:11.

poor rates and additional benevolent societies; others for compulsory laws protective of labor, and fixing a *minimum*, below which it shall be penal to reduce it; while others, and those not the least able to appreciate all the difficulties of the question, have sought the last resource of suffering poverty and oppressed industry in the humanity and sense of justice of the wealthier classes of society. . . .

It were easy to observe, in reply to each and all of the palliatives variously suggested for evils, which none profess to remedy, that to punish crime when committed is not to prevent its commission: to force the work of the poor in poor houses is only farther to glut an already unproductive market; to multiply charities is only to increase pauperism; that to fix by statute the monied price of labor would be impossible in itself, and, if possible, mischievous no less to the laborer than to the employer; and that, under the existing state of things, for human beings, to lean upon the compassion and justice of their fellow creatures, is to lean upon a rotten reed.

I believe no individual, possessed of common sense and common feeling, can have studied the report of the committee to which I have referred, or the multitude of similar documents furnished elsewhere, without acknowledging that reform, and that not slight nor partial, but radical and universal, is called for. All must admit that no such reform—that is, that no remedy commensurate with the evil has been suggested, and would we but reflect, we should perceive that no efficient remedy *can* be suggested, or if suggested, applied, until the people are generally engaged in its discovery and its application for themselves.

In this nation, any more than in any other nation, the mass has never reflected for the mass; the people, as a body, have never addressed themselves to the study of their own condition, and to the just and fair interpretation of their common interests. And, as it was with their national independence, so shall it be with their national happiness—it shall be found only when the mass shall seek it. No people have ever received liberty *in gift*. Given, it were not appreciated; it were not understood. Won without exertion, it were lost as readily. Let the people of America recall the ten years of war and tribulation by which they purchased their national independence. Let efforts as strenuous be now made, not with the sword of steel, indeed, but with the sword of the spirit, and their farther enfranchisement from poverty, starvation, and dependence must be equally successful.

Great reforms are not wrought in a day. Evils which are the accumulated results of accumulated errors, are not to be struck down at a blow by the rod of a magician. A free people may boast that all power is in their hands; but no effectual power can be in their hands until knowledge be in their minds.

But how may knowledge be imparted to their minds? Such effective knowledge as shall render apparent to all the interests of all, and demonstrate the simple truths—that a nation to be strong, must be united; to be united, must be equal in condition; to be equal in condition, must be similar in habits and in feeling; to be similar in habits and in feeling, *must be raised in national institutions as the children of a common family, and citizens of a common country. . . .*

This measure, my friends, has been long present to my mind as befitting the adoption of the American people; as alone calculated to form an enlightened, a virtuous, and a happy community; as alone capable of supplying a remedy to the evils under which we groan; as alone commensurate with the interests of the human family, and consistent with the political institutions of this great confederated republic.

I had occasion formerly to observe, in allusion to the efforts already made, and yet making, in the cause of popular instruction, more or less throughout the Union, that, as yet, the true principle has not been hit; and that until it be hit, all reform must be slow and inefficient.

The noble example of New England has been imitated by other states, until all not possessed of common schools blush for the popular remissness. But, after all, how can *common schools,*[4] under their best form, and in fullest supply, effect even the purpose which they have in view?

The object proposed by common schools (if I rightly understand it) is to impart to the whole population those means for the acquirement of knowledge which are in common use: reading and writing. To these are added arithmetic, and, occasionally perhaps, some imperfect lessons in the simpler sciences. But, I would ask, supposing these institutions should even be made to embrace all the branches of intellectual knowledge, and, thus, science offered gratis to all the children of the land, how are the children of the very class, for whom we suppose the schools instituted, to be supplied with food and raiment, or instructed in the trade necessary to their future subsistence, while they are following these studies? How are they, I ask, to be fed and clothed, when, as all facts show, the labor of the parents is often insufficient for their own sustenance, and, almost universally, inadequate to the provision of the family without the united efforts of all its members? In your manufacturing

[4]*common schools:* public schools akin to those in existence today.

districts you have children worked for twelve hours a day; and, in the rapid and certain progress of the existing system, you will soon have them, as in England, *worked to death,* and yet unable, through the period of their miserable existence, to earn a pittance sufficient to satisfy the cravings of hunger. At this present time, what leisure or what spirit, think you, have the children of the miserable widows of Philadelphia, realizing, according to the most favorable estimate of your city and county committee, sixteen dollars per annum, for food and clothing— what leisure or what spirit may their children find for visiting a school, although the same should be open to them from sunrise to sunset? Or what leisure have usually the children of your most thriving mechanics, after their strength is sufficiently developed to spin, sew, weave, or wield a tool? It seems to me, my friends, that to build school houses nowadays is something like building churches. When you have them, you need some measure to ensure their being occupied. . . .

In lieu of all common schools, high schools, colleges, seminaries, houses of refuge, or any other juvenile institution, instructional or protective, I would suggest that the state legislatures be directed . . . to organize, at suitable distances, and in convenient and healthy situations, establishments for the general reception of all the children resident within the said school district. These establishments to be devoted, severally, to children between a certain age. Say, the first to infants between two and four, or two and six, according to the density of the population, and such other local circumstances as might render a greater or less number of establishments necessary or practicable. The next to receive children from four to eight, or six to twelve years. The next from twelve to sixteen, or to an older age if found desirable. Each establishment to be furnished with instructors in every branch of knowledge, intellectual and operative, with all the apparatus, land, and conveniences necessary for the best developement of all knowledge; the same, whether operative or intellectual, being always calculated to the age and strength of the pupils. . . .

It will be understood that, in the proposed establishments, the children would pass from one to the other in regular succession, and that the parents, who would necessarily be resident in their close neighborhood, could visit the children at suitable hours, but, in no case, interfere with or interrupt the rules of the institution.

In the older establishments, the well directed and well protected labor of the pupil would, in time, suffice for, and, then, exceed, their own support; when the surplus might be devoted to the maintenance of the infant establishments.

In the beginning, and until all debt was cleared off, and so long as the same should be found favorable to the promotion of these best palladiums of a nation's happiness, a double tax might be at once expedient and politic.

First, a moderate tax per head for every child, to be laid upon its parents conjointly or divided between them, due attention being always paid to the varying strength of the two sexes, and to the undue depreciation which now rests on female labor. The more effectually to correct the latter injustice, as well as to consult the convenience of the industrious classes generally, this parental tax might be rendered payable either in money, or in labor, produce, or domestic manufactures, and should be continued for each child until the age when juvenile labor should be found, on the average, equivalent to the educational expenses, which, I have reason to believe, would be at twelve years.

This first tax on parents to embrace equally the whole population; as, however moderate, it would inculcate a certain forethought in all the human family; more especially where it is most wanted—in young persons, who, before they assumed the responsibility of parents, would estimate their fitness to meet it.

The second tax to be on property, increasing in percentage with the wealth of the individual. In this manner I conceive the rich would contribute, according to their riches, to the relief of the poor, and to the support of the state, by raising up its best bulwark—an enlightened and united generation.

Preparatory to, or connected with, such measures, a registry should be opened by the state, with offices through all the townships, where, on the birth of every child, or within a certain time appointed, the same should be entered, together with the names of its parents. When two years old, the parental tax should be payable, and the juvenile institution open for the child's reception; from which time forward it would be under the protective care and guardianship of the state, while it need never be removed from the daily, weekly, or frequent inspection of the parents.

Orphans, of course, would find here an open asylum. If possessed of property, a contribution would be paid from its revenue to the common educational fund; if unprovided, they would be sustained out of the same.

In these nurseries of a free nation, no inequality must be allowed to enter. Fed at a common board; clothed in a common garb, uniting neatness with simplicity and convenience; raised in the exercise of common duties, in the acquirement of the same knowledge and practice of the same industry, varied only according to individual taste and capabilities; in the exercise of the same virtues, in the enjoyment of the same pleasures; in the study of the same nature; in pursuit of the same object—their own and each other's happiness—say! would not such a race, when arrived at manhood and womanhood work out the reform of society—perfect the free institutions of America? . . .

23

MATHEW CAREY

Address to the Wealthy of the Land
1831

One of the early republic's most prominent printers and editors, Mathew Carey (1760–1839) had come to the United States in the 1780s as a political refugee. By the time he was twenty-five, he had already served prison time in England for authoring incendiary Irish nationalist tracts. After fleeing to the United States, Carey quickly became one of Philadelphia's leading publishers. His writings addressed political issues like the Alien and Sedition Acts and the War of 1812, as well as economic matters. In particular, Carey was a strident advocate of protective tariffs— and thus an opponent of the growing number of American and English economists who were advocating free-market policies. That opposition carried into his writings on urban poverty, where he denied the ability of an impartial market to provide a living wage to workers. Carey was especially impassioned in defense of Philadelphia's female seamstresses, whose wages failed to rise to a subsistence level during the city's rampant growth in the early nineteenth century. After evaluating family budgets and speaking to employers and employees alike, Carey offered concrete evidence that the rising tide of the American economy had failed to lift all boats.

Mathew Carey, *Address to the Wealthy of the Land, Ladies as Well as Gentlemen, on the Character, Conduct, Situation, and Prospects, of Those Whose Sole Dependence for Subsistence, Is on the Labour of Their Hands* (Philadelphia: Wm. F. Geddes, 1831).

I propose in these essays to consider and attempt to refute certain pernicious errors that too generally prevail respecting the situation, the conduct, the characters, and the prospects of those whose sole dependence is on the labour of their hands—who comprise, throughout the world, two-thirds, perhaps three-fourths of the human race—and on whose services the other third or fourth depend for their necessaries, their comforts, their enjoyments, and their luxuries. Whatever concerns the comfort or happiness, the morals or the manners of such a large portion of mankind,—whatever tends to increase or decrease the former, or to elevate or depress the latter, is deeply interesting to all whose views extend beyond their own narrow selfish concerns, and who without the services of this class would be forlorn and helpless.

The class in question is susceptible of two great sub-divisions—those who are so well remunerated for their labours, as to be able, not merely to provide, when employed, for seasons of stagnation and sickness, but by industry, prudence, and economy, to save enough in the course of a few years, to commence business on a small scale on their own account. With this fortunate description, which is numerous and respectable, I have no concern at present. My object is to consider the case of those whose services are so inadequately remunerated, owing to the excess of labour beyond the demand for it, that they can barely support themselves while in good health and fully employed, and of course, when sick or unemployed, must perish, unless relieved by charitable individuals, benevolent societies, or the guardians of the poor. I use the word *"perish,"* with due deliberation, and a full conviction of its appropriate application to the case, however revolting it may seem to the reader—for as these people depend for daily support on their daily or weekly wages, they are, when those wages are stopped by whatever means, utterly destitute of wherewith to support their existence, and actually become paupers, and therefore, without the aid above stated, would, I repeat, *"perish"* of want. . . .

The erroneous opinions, to which I alluded in the commencement of this essay, are—

1. That every man, woman, and grown child, able and willing to work, may find employment.
2. That the poor, by industry, prudence, and economy, may at all times support themselves comfortably, without depending on eleemosynary aid—and, as a corollary from these positions,
3. That their sufferings and distresses chiefly, if not wholly, arise from their idleness, their dissipation, and their extravagance.

4. That taxes for the support of the poor, and aid afforded them by charitable individuals or benevolent societies, are pernicious, as, by encouraging the poor to depend on them, they foster their idleness and improvidence, and thus produce, or at least increase the poverty and distress they are intended to relieve.

These opinions, so far as they have operated—and, through the mischievous zeal and industry of the school of political economists, by which they have been promulgated, they have spread widely—have been pernicious to the rich and the poor. They tend to harden the hearts of the former against the sufferings and distresses of the latter,—and of course prolong those sufferings and distresses. Many wealthy individuals, benevolent and liberal, apprehensive lest they might produce evil to society, are, by these doctrines, prevented from indulging

Figure 6.   *Street Hawkers.*

Girls and boys, along with adult women and men, traversed city streets selling matches, fresh fruits and vegetables, cloth and ribbons, and prepared foods. Petty marketing was arduous labor but provided women and African Americans with some of their only opportunities for self-employment. Street vendors plied their wares with distinctive "cries"—songs, rhymes, or chants that would be recognizable to anyone hearing them. These cries were often collected in small books depicting urban life, although the editors added moral homilies as well.

Cries of Philadelphia (Philadelphia: Johnson and Warner, 1810), 16–17. The Historical Society of Pennsylvania (HSP), *Cries of Philadelphia* [Am 1810 Cri].

the feelings of their hearts, and employing a portion of their superfluous wealth, for the best purpose to which it can be appropriated—that purpose, which, at the hour of death, will afford the most solid comfort on retrospection—that is, "to feed the hungry; to give drink to the thirsty; to clothe the naked; to comfort the comfortless." The economists in question, when they are implored by the starving poor for "bread," tender them "a stone." To the unfeeling and uncharitable of the rich (and such unhappily there are,) these doctrines afford a plausible pretext, of which they are not slow to avail themselves, to withhold their aid from the poor. They have moreover tended to attach a sort of disrepute to those admirable associations of ladies and gentlemen, for the relief of the poor, on which Heaven looks down with complacence, and which form a delightful oasis in the midst of the arid deserts of sordid selfishness which on all sides present themselves to the afflicted view of the contemplative observer.

I. So far as regards the first position which I have undertaken to combat, it will scarcely be denied by any candid person, that in the most prosperous times and countries, there are certain occupations, which, by the influence of fashion or other causes, suffer occasional stagnations. There are other occupations at which employment is at all times precarious—and others again, which furnish little or no employment at certain seasons of the year.

To the first class belong all those who minister to the fanciful wants of society—wants contracted or expanded by the whim or caprice of fashion. For instance, the king of England or the Prince of Wales having, some years since, laid aside his shoe-buckles, and supplied their place with ribands,[1] shoe-buckles became unfashionable, and the journeymen buckle-makers were reduced to a state approaching to starvation. . . .

In the second class, the most conspicuous are the spoolers, and seamstresses employed on coarse work,[2] who, being far more numerous than the demand for their service requires, a portion of them are at all times but partially employed.

In the third class may be enumerated labourers on canals and turnpike roads, hod carriers,[3] wood sawyers, wood pilers, &c. &c.

Instances repeatedly occur in our cities, of decent men, with the most satisfactory recommendations, seeking employment in vain for months, as porters. There is at all times a superabundance of clerks.

---

[1] *ribands:* ribbons.
[2] *coarse work:* the least skilled sewing, usually inexpensive ready-to-wear clothing.
[3] *hod carriers:* men who carry bricks and mortar to masons.

An advertisement for a person of this class, will, in an hour or two, produce a dozen or two of applications. I have known persons of this description, burdened with families, obliged to descend to menial and degrading employments for support.

It is frequently said, as a panacea for the distresses of those people—"Let them go into the country. There they will find employment enough." To say nothing of the utter unfitness of most of those persons for country labour, this is taking for granted, what remains to be proved. The country rarely affords employment for extra hands, except for a few weeks in the harvest. Farmers are generally supplied with steady hands at all other seasons. But were it otherwise, take the case of a man of a weakly constitution, with a wife and three or four small children; what a miserable chance would he stand of support by country labour!

So far as regards seamstresses and spoolers, the employment of the two classes, through the year, does not average above 40 [to] 45 weeks. One thousand of the former have been employed by the Providence Society[4] in this city, during a winter, who could procure only four shirts per week, for which they received but fifty cents! Some of them, living two miles from the office, had to travel four miles for this paltry pittance—and above half of them had no other dependence. In the absence of all other evidence, this would be abundantly sufficient to establish the cruelty and injustice of the accusations brought against this ill-fated and oppressed class, when they are involved in the general censure passed on the poor for idleness and improvidence.

On the second and third opinions; a few facts will suffice to convince the most sceptical of their destitution of foundation.

A primary element in this discussion is a consideration of the wages ordinarily paid to the class of persons whose case I attempt to develope, and whose cause I have undertaken to plead—and first, of the very numerous class, labourers on canals and turnpikes.

. . . [I]t appears that the average wages of this class in common times, are from ten to twelve dollars per month and found;[5] that in winter they may be had for five dollars; and that sometimes in that season, when labour is scarce, they work for their board alone. . . .

It is important to observe, that in this and similar cases, averages do not afford a fair criterion to form a correct decision. This may at

---

[4] *the Providence Society:* a private charity that distributed cloth to poor women and purchased the finished products.

[5] *found:* room and board.

first glance appear unsound doctrine, but a very slight reflection will remove all doubt on the subject. Suppose A and B to work, the one at seven dollars and the other at ten—the average would be eight and a half. But would it be fair to calculate the capacity of A to support his family by this average? Surely not. The calculation must be made on his actual wages: I will therefore assume ten dollars for ten months, and five dollars for two—and take the case of a labourer with a wife and two children. Many of them have three and four.

10 Months at 10 Dollars,	$100 00
2 Months at 5 Dollars,	10 00
Suppose the wife to earn half a dollar per week,	26 00
Total,	136 00

I now submit a calculation of the expenses of such a family, every item of which is at a low rate.

Shoes and clothes for self and wife, each 12 dollars,	$24 00
Washing at the canal, 12½ cents per week,	6 50
Shoes and clothes for two children, each 8 dollars	16 00
Rent 50 cents per week	26 00
Soap, candles, &c. 6 cents per week	3 12
Fuel, 15 cents per week,	7 80
Meat, drink, vegetables, &c. &c. 8 cents per day, each, for wife and children,	87 60
	$171 02
Deficit,	$35 02

This is one of a large class, whom some of our political economists of the new school, are not ashamed to stigmatize as worthless and improvident, because they do not, forsooth, save enough out of their miserable wages, to support themselves and families, in times of scarcity, without the aid of benevolent societies; whereas it appears that their wages are inadequate to their support, even when fully employed.

Here, let it be observed, there is no allowance for a single day in the whole year lost by accident, by sickness, or by want of employment— no allowance for expense arising from sickness of wife or children—no allowance for the contingency ... of working, during the winter months, for board alone. It is assumed that no unfavourable circumstance has taken place—that every thing has "run on with a smooth current," and yet the man's earnings and those of his wife fall short of their support $35!!!

But we will present the case in another point of view. Suppose him to have $12 per month for ten months—and $5 for two—that his wife earns half a dollar per week—that neither of them loses a day by sickness or otherwise—and let us see the result.

10 months at $12 each,	$120
2 [months] at $5	10
Wife's earnings per week, 50 cents	21
	$156
Expenditure as before,	$171

Even on this supposition he falls short 15 dollars a year of a meagre support; what an overwhelming commentary on the idle and vapid declamations against the improvidence of the poor! and what an irresistible argument in favour of benevolent societies! . . .

Calculations respecting city labourers, hod men, wood pilers, scavengers, and various other classes, whose sole dependence is on the casual employment of their hands, are attended with considerable difficulty. I have made inquiries of different persons, particularly of master-builders, as regards labourers and hod men. Their statements vary extremely. One eminent builder, who employs a number of hands, states that allowing for occasional heavy rains, in spring, summer, and fall, and the partial suspension of building in winter, those persons are not sure of employment more than 200 days in the year.—This appears to be quite too low. Another, who states that wages vary from 25 to 37½ cents per day in winter, and to 62½, 75, 87½ and 100 cents, in spring, summer and fall, assumes an average of 60 cents per day throughout the year. This again is apparently too low. Be this as it may, whatever the wages assumed of the various estimates, it will be manifest that the most rigid economy will not secure persons of the description in question from occasional distress, in the event of any of the calamities to which they are subject, that is, accidents, sickness, or want of employment, &c.

I do not pretend my calculations are strictly accurate. They are however a sufficiently near approximation, to satisfy every candid mind of the enormous and pernicious errors which prevail on this subject.

When a labourer has a wife and only one child; or neither one nor the other, he undoubtedly fares well, and does not fall within the scope of this essay. When, on the other hand, he has a sickly wife and three or four or five children, and is himself occasionally sick, his case is truly deplorable; and many of them have four, five, and six children. Their children are, I believe, generally more numerous than those of the rich.

I might extend these views to greater lengths, and embrace various other occupations, which stand on nearly the same ground as those I have specified. But I presume it cannot be necessary; and hope I have established a point of infinite importance to the poor, and highly interesting to the rich—that is, that even among the occupations of males, there are some, which are so indifferently remunerated, that no industry—no economy—no providence, in times when the parties are fully employed, will enable them to save wherewith to support themselves and families in times of stagnation and during severe seasons; and that of course they must rely, on those occasions, upon the overseers of the poor, or benevolent societies, or charitable individuals, or on such extraordinary aid as, to the honor of our citizens, the late distressing scenes called forth. If I succeed in deeply imprinting this important truth on the public mind, so that it may produce the proper effect, by removing the injurious prejudices that prevail on the conduct and character of the labouring poor, on the effects of benevolent societies, and on the claims of those societies for extensive support, I shall regard myself as signally fortunate. . . .

Let it not be for a moment supposed, that I carry my defence of the poor to such an extravagant and ill-judged length, as to contend that all their distresses and sufferings arise from inadequate wages, or that they are all faultless. Far from it. I know there are among them, as among all other classes, worthless persons—and some supremely worthless. Among the heavy sins of this class is that of desertion by some of them, of their wives and children, or, what is equally bad, living in a state of idleness on the earnings of their wives. Indeed so far as regards their ill-fated partners, the latter course is the worse. In the one case, the husband only withdraws his aid—in the other, he not only commits that offence, but adds to the burdens of his wife.

I venture to assert that so far as regards the sexes, among the poor, there are twice as many worthless males as females—idle, dissipated and intemperate. The females are, with few exceptions, orderly, regular, and industrious, and husband their slender means with exemplary economy—an economy without which they would frequently suffer from hunger.

From the most attentive examination of the subject, I am fully satisfied that the worthless of both sexes bear but a small proportion to those who are industrious and meritorious. Unfortunately the worthless occupy a more prominent space in the public eye, and with many are unceasing objects of animadversion and reprobation—their numbers and their follies and vices are magnified; whereas the industrious are always in the back ground, out of view.

The industry of the labouring poor appears undeniable from the fact, that there is no occupation, however deleterious or disgraceful, at which there is any difficulty in procuring labourers, even at inadequate wages. The labour on canals in marsh situations, in atmospheres, replete with pestilential miasmata,[6] is full proof on this point. Although the almost certain consequence of labouring in such situations, is a prostration of health, and danger of life—and that no small portion of the labourers return to their families in the fall or winter with health and vigour destroyed, and labouring under protracted fevers and agues, which in many cases undermine their constitutions, and return in after years, and, as I have already stated, too often hurry them prematurely into eternity—their places are readily supplied by other victims who offer themselves upon the altars of industry.

This is one of those decisive facts which ought to silence cavil for ever on this important subject.

Let us now return to the appalling case of seamstresses, employed on coarse work, and to that of spoolers, and here "I will a tale unfold," "to harrow up the soul," of all those endowed with feelings of humanity.

Coarse shirts, and duck pantaloons, are frequently made for 8, and 10 cents. The highest rate in the United States...is 12½ cents. Women free from the incumbrance of children, in perfect health, and with constant uninterrupted employment, cannot, by the testimony of ladies of the first respectability, who have fully scrutinized the affair, make more than nine shirts per week, working from twelve to fifteen hours per day, and possessing considerable expertness. Those incumbered with children, or in indifferent health, or inexpert, cannot make more than six or seven. They are, moreover, as I have already stated, very partially employed. But laying aside all the various disadvantages and drawbacks, and placing the circumstances in the most favorable point of light, let us consider the case of a woman in perfect health, without children, and with uninterrupted employment—and see the result of her painful labours, and how little attention is paid to the awful denunciation against those that *"grind the faces of the poor."*

---

[6]*miasmata:* vapor believed to cause diseases like yellow fever.

9 shirts per week = 1.12½. Per annum,		$58 50
Rent at 50 cents,	26 00	
Clothes, suppose,	10 00	
Fuel per week, say 15 cents,	7 80	
Soap, candles, &c. 4 cents,	2 08	
Remain for food and drink 24 cents per week, or about 3½ cents per day !!!!!! }	12 62	
		$58 50

But suppose the woman to have one or two children; to work for ten cents; to be a part of her time unemployed—say one day in each week—and to make, of course, six, but say seven shirts.

7 shirts, or 70 cents per week, is per annum,		$36 40
Rent, fuel, soap, candles, &c. as before,	$45 88	
Deficit,	9 48	
		$36 40

Such is the hideous, the deplorable state of a numerous and interesting portion of the population of our cities in the most prosperous country in the world! And be it noted, to the discredit of the wealthy portion of the nation, of both sexes, particularly the ladies, that this subject has for three years been pressed on the public attention in almost every shape and form, without exciting a single efficient effort in Boston, New York, or Philadelphia—I will not say, to remedy or alleviate this horrible state of things—but even to inquire into it, and ascertain whether it was or was not remediless! It is impossible to regard this apathy without exciting the utmost astonishment.

I have not lightly thrown a higher degree of censure on the ladies in this case, than on the gentlemen. It was peculiarly the cause of the former. Their sex are "ground to the earth" and it was the peculiar duty and province of the ladies to stand forth in their defence. In such a holy cause of humanity their efforts could not have failed of success. They might readily have stimulated their fathers, brothers, husbands and cousins, to meet and devise some plan to mitigate sufferings, which drive numbers of unfortunate women to DESTRUCTION—to ruin[7] here, and perhaps hereafter. Half the zeal, the effort that they make in other causes, not calling so loudly for their interference, would have sufficed to render the defence of those oppressed women fashionable. But

[7] *ruin:* a euphemistic term for prostitution.

they have looked on with calm indifference. Application on the subject has been made in Philadelphia and New York, personally or by letter, to above fifty ladies in each city—and every one of them expressed deep sympathy for the sufferers, but the sympathy was barren and unproductive.

In speaking of the effect on some of those unfortunate women, to drive them to licentious courses, I ought to use the strongest language the subject would admit of, in order to make a deep impression on the reader, somewhat commensurate with the magnitude of the evil, and the enormity of the oppression under which they groan. A due consideration of their actual situation, and the gloomy prospects before them, would lead to anticipate such a result. Beset on the one side, by poverty and wretchedness—with scanty and poor fare; miserable lodgings; clothing inferior in quality and often inadequate in quantity; without the most distant hope of a melioration of condition, by a course of honest and unremitting industry—and on the other side, the allurements of present enjoyments; comfortable apartments; fine dress; with a round of pleasures: all these held out by vice and crime to entice them from the paths of virtue, is it wonderful that many of them fall victims, and enter on the "broad path that leads to destruction?" Is not the trial almost too severe for poor human nature?[8] ...

But we are gravely told, that these women ought to go to service[9]—that servants are scarce; if they would condescend to fill that station, they might have comfortable homes; abundance of good food; light labour, and high wages. . . .

But be this as it may, I would observe that among the class of persons depending on sewing and spooling, there is a large proportion of aged widows, who are wholly unfit for service, and there are among them many young widows, with two or three small children, who are as dear to them, as theirs are to the rich—whom, of course, they cannot bear to part with; and whom their wages, as servants, would not enable them to support at nurse.

---

[8]Carey printed a footnote containing several letters linking low wages to prostitution. One will suffice here:
  Extract of a letter from Dr. Van Rensselaer, of New York.
"My profession affords me many and unpleasant opportunities of knowing the wants of those unfortunate females, who try to earn an honest subsistence by the needle, and to witness the struggles often made by honest pride and destitution. *I could cite many instances of young, and even middle-aged women, who have been 'lost to virtue,' apparently by no other cause than the lowness of wages, and* THE ABSOLUTE IMPOSSIBILITY OF PROCURING THE NECESSARIES OF LIFE BY HONEST INDUSTRY."
  [9]*to go to service:* to work as domestic servants.

The pernicious consequences of the inadequate wages paid the women of the classes in question, is strikingly displayed by the state of the out-door paupers in the city of Philadelphia. Of 498 females, there are

Seamstresses,	142
Washerwomen,	62
Spoolers,	28
Shoe-binders,	10
	—— 242.

Being nearly one-half of the whole number. There are 406 widows.

It may excite wonder how the seamstresses, spoolers, &c. are able to support human nature, as their rent absorbs above two-fifths of their miserable earnings. The fact is, they generally contrive to raise their rent by begging from benevolent citizens, and of course their paltry earnings go to furnish food and clothing.

. . . The fourth position which I undertook to controvert, is, that

"Taxes for the support of the poor, and aid afforded them by benevolent societies and charitable individuals, are pernicious; as, by encouraging the poor to depend on them, they foster their idleness and improvidence, and thus produce, or at least increase the poverty and distress they are intended to relieve."

If I have proved, as I hope I have satisfactorily, that there are classes of people, male and female, whose dependence is on their hands for support, and whose wages, when fully employed, are not more than sufficient for that purpose; that when unemployed, they must be reduced to penury and want; and that there are classes of females, whose wages are inadequate for their support, even when constantly employed; it follows, of course, that the poor rates, the aid of benevolent societies, &c. far from producing the pernicious effects ascribed to them, are imperiously necessary, and that without them, numbers would actually perish of want, as I have stated, or would have recourse to mendicity;[10] and mendicants impose a far heavier tax on a community than the same number of paupers, supported by poor rates. The support of the 549 out-door paupers of Philadelphia averages 46¼ cents per week—or less than 7 cents per day. Some of them

---

[10]*mendicity:* street begging.

receive only a quarter dollar a week. I submit a statement of the whole number, with the pittance they respectively receive:—

42	@	25 cents.
2	@	31¼
186	@	37½
259	@	50
17	@	62½
42	@	75
1	@	100
549		

If these were strolling mendicants, as, by the abrogation of the poor laws, and the annihilation of benevolent societies, they would become, the average, instead of seven cents per day, would more probably be 25 or 30 cents, thus increasing the burdens on the community three or four fold. Many of them, with a woe-begone appearance, whether real or fictitious, calculated to excite sympathy, would probably realize 50 cents, and often a dollar a day.

Those of our fellow-citizens who complain of the oppression of our poor laws, will learn with surprize, that of the 549 out-door paupers, there are no less than 390 above 60 years of age, and 6 above 100.— Almost all of these are in a state of superannuation, 50 of them are blind, and 406 of the whole number, as I have already stated, are widows. ...

24

The Manayunk Working People's Committee

1833

Mechanization accounted for the boom in American textile manufacturing in the 1820s and 1830s. Although mills offered jobs to men, women, and children alike, wages and working conditions were hardly ideal. Manayunk was the center of textile production in the Philadelphia region,

Pennsylvanian, August 28, 1833. Reprinted in John R. Commons et al., eds., *A Documentary History of American Industrial Society* (Cleveland: Arthur H. Clark, 1910), 5:330–33.

and critics compared it unfavorably to Manchester—the dismal English manufacturing city. Instead of making the lives of workers easier, the new mill technology seemed to turn humans into machines. Grueling hours, dangerous conditions, and low wages led to serious disenchantment for mill workers, who emulated skilled artisans by organizing themselves politically and bringing their grievances before the public. For laborers throughout the country, a ten-hour workday had become a standard demand. Workers insisted upon the extra hours in the day for self-improvement and political activity, much to the dismay and fear of their employers.

FELLOW CITIZENS:

Deeply impressed with a sense of our inability to combat single-handed the evils that now threaten us, and being fully convinced, that the future happiness of ourselves and families depend on our present exertions, we are, with reluctance, obliged to lay our grievances and petition before you, well knowing that we are appealing to an enlightened and generous public. We therefore submit the following, with all the candor of feeling with which the human mind is capable of expressing itself, and may you judge us according to our merits.

We are obliged by our employers to labor at this season of the year, from 5 o'clock in the morning until sunset, being fourteen hours and a half, with an intermission of half an hour for breakfast, and an hour for dinner, leaving thirteen hours of hard labor, at an unhealthy employment, where we never feel a refreshing breeze to cool us, overheated and suffocated as we are, and where we never behold the sun but through a window, and an atmosphere thick with the dust and small particles of cotton, which we are constantly inhaling to the destruction of our health, our appetite, and strength.

Often do we feel ourselves so weak as to be scarcely able to perform our work, on account of the overstrained time we are obliged to labor through the long and sultry days of summer, in the impure and unwholesome air of the factories, and the little rest we receive during the night not being sufficient to recruit our exhausted physical energies, we return to our labor in the morning, as weary as when we left it; but nevertheless work we must, worn down and debilitated as we are, or our families would soon be in a starving condition, for our wages are barely sufficient to supply us with the necessaries of life. We cannot provide against sickness or difficulties of any kind, by laying by a single dollar, for our present wants consume the little we receive, and when we are confined to a bed of sickness any length of time, we are plunged into the deepest distress, which often terminates in total ruin, poverty and pauperism.

Our expenses are perhaps greater than most other working people, because it requires the wages of all the family who are able to work, (save only one small girl to take care of the house and provide meals) to furnish absolute wants, consequently the females have no time either to make their own dresses or those of the children, but have of course to apply to trades for every article that is wanted.

"The laborer is worthy of his hire," is a maxim acknowledged to be true in theory by all, and yet how different is the practice. Are we not worthy of our hire? Most certainly we are, and yet our employers would wish to reduce our present wages twenty per cent! and tell us their reason for so doing is, that cotton has risen in value, but is it not a necessary consequence of the rise of cotton that cotton goods will rise also; and what matters it to us what the price of cotton is, our wants are as great when cotton is dear as they are when it is cheap; if our employers make more profit on their goods at any one time than they do at others, they do not give us better wages, and is it justice that we should bear all the burthen and submit to a reduction of our wages? No, we could not consistently with our duty to ourselves and to each other, submit to it, and rivet our chains still closer! We have long suffered the evils of being divided in our sentiments, but the universal oppressions that we now all feel, have roused us to a sense of our oppressed condition, and we are now determined to be oppressed no longer! We know full well that the attempted reduction in our wages is but the forerunner of greater evils, and greater oppressions, which would terminate, if not resisted, in slavery.

When we look around us, and see the cheerful faces, the happy homes, and many comforts and conveniences of life, which others enjoy; we cannot but feel the disadvantages under which we labor, in our present reduced situation. Where is the man who would change situations with us, after viewing us, and the tyranny by which we are oppressed? There is not one! The hardy workman who labors upon the public roads, breathing the pure air of heaven and enjoying more perfect happiness and liberty than we do—would say, "Give me my sun burnt features, my health and strength, in preference to the pale cheek, the sunken eye, and emaciated form that manufacturers exhibit!"

The deplorable condition of the children working in the factories of England, has been represented in glowing colors, and their burthens alleviated—but what has been done for ours? Nothing! Although our children are oppressed as much as those in the English factories, there has been but few to vindicate their rights, or redress their wrongs; but we hope that every good feeling person will assist us in relieving them of their present burthens.

They are obliged at a very early age to enter the factories, to contribute to the support of the family—by which means they are reared in total ignorance of the world, and the consequence of that ignorance, is the inculcation of immoral and oftentimes vicious habits, which terminates in the disgrace of many of them in public prisons. When on the other hand, if we were relieved of our present oppressions—a reasonable time for labor established, and wages adequate to our labors allowed us, we might then live comfortable, and place our children at some public school, where they might receive instruction sufficient to carry them with propriety through life. But situated as they are, and reared in ignorance, they are trampled upon by every ambitious knave who can boast of a long purse, and made the tools of political as well as avaricious men, who lord it over them as does the southern planter over his slaves!

The female part of the hands employed in the factories are subject to the same burthens that we are, without the least allowance made on the part of our employers, for their sex or age—they must labor as we do, and suffer as we do; and those of them who are grown to womanhood, can barely support themselves by their industry.

We have here drawn but a faint sketch of the oppressions we labor under, but we hope by this to induce the public to examine for themselves. It would be endless to point out in detail, all the injustice we suffer from an overbearing aristocracy, but all that we have here stated are facts which cannot be denied.

25

PHILADELPHIA NATIONAL LABORER

On Wage Slavery

1836

As capitalist labor relations intensified in northern cities in the 1830s, militant artisans began to describe themselves as "wage slaves." The republican identities of white northern workers had always stemmed from the fact that despite working with their hands, they were not degraded like slaves. Hence, to say that capitalists were turning them into slaves was powerful rhetoric. But this language had unintended consequences, which southern ideologues seized to fend off abolitionist attacks: Northern workers were not only slaves, but they were worse off than Southern slaves who received cradle-to-grave welfare from their owners. In contrast, the exploitative northern system treated workers like machines, broke their bodies, and cast their hollow remains on the government to care for. Obviously, the similarities between slaves and wage laborers could be overstated, and there are no records of Northern workers selling themselves into slavery for better treatment. Nonetheless, standards of worker welfare became an important benchmark as northerners and southerners contrasted their societies in the 1830s and beyond.

A southern planter possesses five hundred slaves: he acquired them by inheritance, or purchased them with his money. He claims their perpetual services; and the laws of his country sanction his claim. By his powerful exertions, or by a fortunate occurrence of circumstances, he has acquired an absolute ascendency over these men: consequently they are absolutely his slaves.

A northern farmer is in possession of a landed estate, worth one hundred thousand dollars. His fields are cultivated by fifty or sixty ragged miserable laborers; to which he gives twelve dollars a month one year, because they cannot be procured at a cheaper rate. Another year, laborers are numerous; they range over the country in every direction begging for employment. He now hires them for ten, eight, seven, six, five, four, dollars a month, and even sometimes allows them nothing (to make use of a favorite expression of his own) but

"Sarage," *Philadelphia National Laborer,* April 9, 1836.

ENGLAND.

Oh heaven, I in this horried band of freedom to be starving for want of employment. As relief from the parsimual arcocracy whose bloated for labor have been made by our blood and toil.'

Come pack off to the work house! that's the only life as fum for you!

AMERICA.

God bless you massa, you find and cloth us. When we are sick you nurse us and when too old to work you provide for us.'

These poor creatures are a sacred legacy from my ancestors and while is dollars left me, nothing shall be spared to increase their comfort and happiness *their victuals for their work.* Observe well, that he exercises every power, which his own exertions, or a fortunate concurrence of circumstances, have given him over his fellow men.

What injustice is discoverable in the conduct of the southern planter, which is not also found in the practices of the northern farmer? They are both *tyrants* to the utmost of their abilities. They both hold their fellow creatures in *slavery* as unbounded as their powers. Nor is the condition of the white slave in the northern states much preferable to that of the black slave in the southern parts of the Union. The laws and the progress of civilization have made the indigent laborer a slave to every man in possession of riches. He may change his master; but he is condemned to perpetual servitude; and his reward is the reward of every other slave—*subsistence.* The situation of the white slave is often more unfortunate than that of the black; he is probably harassed by domestic cares, and compelled to be a helpless witness of the distresses of his family; or he changes his employer so often, with the vain hope of meliorating his condition, that he becomes sick, infirm, or old, without having had it in his power to secure the friendship or protection of any of his masters. What then is the consequence? The wretched outcast, after a life of slavery, is neglected by those who have enjoyed the fruit of his labor, he may perish in the streets, expire on the highway, or linger out a miserable existence in some infirmary or poorhouse, till death shall relieve him of his pain, and the world of a burthen. And the pitiful assistance, which is granted, by the rich, to their sick, decrepit, or superannuated slave, is given as a *charity,* accompanied with reproaches and expressions of contempt; and the dying pauper must receive it with all becoming humility. He is upbraided with his vices, reproached with his follies, and unfeelingly insulted by every purseproud fool who may manage the concerns, or have the superintendence, of the poor. The black slave is compelled to labor; but he is destitute of care. He is not at liberty to change one service for another; but he may, by long and faith-

---

Figure 7   (opposite)   *Slave Labor and Wage Labor.*
Relief officials and moral reformers regularly dismissed the complaints of impoverished Northern wage earners by insisting that American workers were less exploited than either English factory operatives or African American slaves. But Northern workers attempted to turn these comparisons to their own advantage by calling themselves "wage slaves" and suggesting that Southern slaves were better off than themselves or their English peers. Although abolitionists rejected such logic, pro-slavery southerners were eager to agree that slavery was a kinder system than free-labor capitalism.
"Chattel Slavery and Wage Slavery" (New York: A. Donnelly, 1844). Collection of The New-York Historical Society.

ful adherence to his labor, secure the affections of his master, and, by assiduous attentions, conciliate his superiors. When he grows old or infirm, he is sure of being maintained, without having recourse to the tender mercies of a justice of the peace, overseer of the poor, or superintendent of a work-house.

Is it not a little strange that the opulent man when he contributes his quota to the necessities of a wretch who has been, in every sense of the word, a slave to the community of the rich, considers himself as bestowing a *charity;* whereas the slaveholder supposes himself bound *in justice* to support the blacks who are worn out in his service? Is it not a little strange that we should hear men in the middle and northern states pour forth reproaches against their brethren to the southward for holding slaves, when they themselves are supported by the labor of slaves? "Thou hypocrite! first cast the beam out of thine own eye; and then shalt thou see clearly to cast the mote out of thy brother's eye."—

SARAGE

A Chronology of Welfare Reform
(1788–1840)

1788 Philadelphia's municipal government retakes control of the city's poor-relief administration, ending a twenty-year experiment with privatization through the Quaker-led Bettering House.

1790 The first federal census finds twenty-four urban areas in the United States (defined as having a population greater than 2,500 residents). No city is larger than 50,000.

1791 Serving the Elector of Bavaria, the American-born Count Rumford orchestrates the arrest of all vagrants and paupers in Munich and institutionalizes them in a school of industry. American writers frequently invoke Rumford's example as they call for new relief policies between 1800 and 1820.

1792 Alexander Hamilton and his allies open a manufacturing village in Paterson, New Jersey, with hopes of marshaling the labor of women and children on behalf of American industry. The first American water-powered textile mill is established the following year in Pawtucket, Rhode Island.

1797 In New York, women found the Society for the Relief of Poor Widows with Small Children. Baltimore women start the Female Humane Association.

The Friendly Society of St. Thomas's African Church in Philadelphia becomes one of the first mutual aid associations for African Americans.

Thomas Paine, author of *Common Sense,* publishes a short pamphlet, *Agrarian Justice,* calling for the government to provide a one-time payment to every person upon reaching the age of twenty-one and an annual payment to every person fifty and older.

1798 The Quaker women of Philadelphia's Female Society for the Relief and Employment of the Poor (founded 1795) open a house of industry for poor women. The small institution offers baby-sitting so that mothers do not need to leave their children unattended while working. This may be the first day-care program provided by an employer in the United States.

In New York, Quaker women start the inelegantly titled Female Association for the Relief of the Sick Poor, and for the Education of Such Female Children as Do Not Belong to, or Are Not Provided for, by Any Religious Society.

Thomas Malthus publishes *An Essay on the Principle of Population,* arguing that population growth, which he attributed to the lack of sexual self-restraint among the poor, would outstrip food supplies and yield starvation, epidemic, and war.

1800   The population of New York City reaches 60,000, and Philadelphia's tops 40,000. Mexico City, the largest city in North America, numbers 130,000. In Europe, London's population approaches 900,000, and Paris's 550,000.

1803   New York Mayor Edward Livingston starts a controversy when he proposes a school of industry to teach craft skills to the poor. Artisans protest that their professional status and wage rates will be undercut and their livelihoods threatened. The plan is scrapped.

A female charity school opens in Fredericksburg, Virginia. Similar asylums for female orphans and poor girls soon open in Norfolk (1804), Richmond (1807), and Petersburg (1813).

President Thomas Jefferson purchases the Louisiana Territory from France and doubles the area of the United States. Jefferson envisions the new lands as a republican antidote to urbanization, industrialization, and the emergence of a landless laboring class.

1804   The Maryland legislature passes a vagrancy law for Baltimore. Besides the homeless and the unemployed, targets include "every woman who is generally reputed a common prostitute, and every juggler, or fortune teller, or common gambler." Those convicted must post a bond pledging a year of good behavior or else serve a nine-month term of labor at the Baltimore almshouse.

1807   The Embargo Act on international commerce undermines maritime trade and creates high unemployment in American seaports, but the disappearance of European imports creates new opportunities for American manufacturing.

1808   The Adelphi School opens for poor boys in Philadelphia. Supporters consider the school "among the best remedies for eradicating vice, and inseparable misery, which unhappily abound."

1809   Leading African American citizens of Philadelphia form a Society for the Suppression of Vice and Immorality to encourage respectable behavior among working-class blacks.

1810   The census finds forty-six urban areas (defined as cities of 2,500 or more residents) in the United States, yet 93 percent of the population lives elsewhere.

Ezra Stiles Ely begins to minister to the sick and needy in the New York almshouse and hospital. To support his ministry, Ely publishes *A Sermon for the Rich to Buy That They May Benefit Themselves and the Poor.*

1811 Maryland's new penitentiary opens in Baltimore. Over the next decade, nearly 200 people—primarily women—will serve year-long terms for vagrancy.

New York City breaks ground on the Bellevue complex—an almshouse, penitentiary, workhouse, and two hospitals on several acres. Despite the use of convict labor, building costs by 1816 will exceed $400,000.

1813 Massachusetts Society for the Suppression of Intemperance is founded.

1814 The Association for the Relief of Respectable, Aged, Indigent Females is founded in New York to assist older women who had formerly been in comfortable circumstances.

The Boston Asylum for Indigent Boys opens for youngsters ages three to twelve. The founders hope "to rescue the most abject and forlorn, as well as those in a state of vagrancy who, roaming from their parents, although young in years, become old in the crimes of stealing, swearing, and lying."

The end of the War of 1812 reopens the United States to British imports and undermines nascent American manufacturing.

1816 The New York Female Missionary Society is founded to proselytize the urban poor. The Boston Society for the Moral and Religious Instruction of the Poor begins its work the next year. The American Bible Society begins printing copies of the New Testament for free distribution.

1817 The Pennsylvania Society for the Promotion of Public Economy forms to stem the rising costs of poor relief in Philadelphia.

The Maryland legislature approves a lottery to raise funds for a house of industry in Baltimore. Moral reformers note the irony of using state-sanctioned gambling to benefit an institution meant to teach the poor the value of hard labor.

1818 The New York Society for the Prevention of Pauperism is founded.

1819 Economic panic creates massive unemployment in cities and manufacturing centers. The economy remains sluggish through 1823.

The Female Hebrew Benevolent Society of Philadelphia is founded, becoming the first Jewish women's benevolent association in the United States.

1820 New York City's population exceeds 120,000, but only 7 percent of Americans live in cities with more than 2,500 residents.

The Boston Society for the Religious and Moral Instruction of the Poor, which opens Sunday schools and seamen's churches and delivers Bibles to the impoverished, gains corporate status from the state of Massachusetts.

William Ellery Channing organizes a conference of fellow liberal ministers to pursue the Unitarian creed of perfectionism, free will, and the power of human reason. This break from orthodox Calvinist belief in inherent human sinfulness and predestination inspires countless reform efforts.

1821 A Massachusetts investigation of the state's poor laws finds that outdoor relief is inefficient and morally harmful. Identifying intemperance as the leading cause of poverty, the committee proposes making all public relief contingent upon entering an almshouse. Based on the report's logic, Boston opens a house of industry to put the able-bodied poor to work for their own support.

New York State abolishes the property requirement for white adult male voters (while raising the property minimum for black male voters). Most northern states now allow adult white male suffrage, giving working-class white men a newfound voice in electoral politics.

1822 A fire tears through the Philadelphia Orphan House, killing 23 of its 91 children. Later that year, Philadelphia Quakers found the Association for the Care of Coloured Orphans, "for where do we find, even in populous cities, a class of the human family more abject, or more deserving of the fostering hand of benevolence, than the parentless child of the African race in this country?"

New York City begins using the stepping-mill to extract labor from vagrants and other criminals housed at the Bellevue facility.

1824 New York secretary of state John Yates publishes a massive report on poor relief, with data from every county. Collectively, local governments are spending nearly $500,000 annually on out-relief and institutionalization.

1825 The New York House of Refuge opens its doors. Boston opens a similar institution the following year, Philadelphia in 1828.

In New York, the Society for the Encouragement of Faithful Domestic Servants begins to offer rewards to household workers who stay with the same employer for more than one year. Officers screen the moral character of domestic servants before placing them in the service of the society's patrons. A similar society opens in Philadelphia in 1829.

The American Tract Society begins publishing short stories of Christian piety for distribution among the poor.

1826 The American Temperance Society is founded in Boston, fresh on the heels of Lyman Beecher's powerful *Six Sermons on the Nature, Occasions, Signs, Evils, and Remedy of Intemperance.*

Also in Boston, Reverend Joseph Tuckerman becomes the Unitarian Church's minister at large to the poor.

1827 Skilled craftsmen in Philadelphia found the Mechanics' Union of Trade Associations, sparking a decade of labor agitation and the emergence of workingmen's political parties in cities throughout the nation.

In response to a report finding that Philadelphia's poor-relief system was less efficient than any other city's, a citizens' committee calls for a streamlined system of relief administration and the erection of a new $220,000 almshouse.

1828   Philadelphia begins eliminating outdoor relief, doing away with cash pensions, and subjecting relief applicants to careful screening.

In Boston, the Infant School Society begins offering day care for the young children of working mothers.

1829   Thomas Skidmore publishes *The Rights of Man to Property!* and Frances Wright galvanizes audiences with her lectures on behalf of the working class.

Mathew Carey heads a Philadelphia committee studying the causes and consequences of low wages for women. A prominent printer, Carey publishes numerous pamphlets calling for increased charity and higher wages for workers.

1830   Reverend Joseph Tuckerman wins a $100 prize from Carey for the best essay on the subject of women's wages and poverty. Both Carey and Tuckerman link low wages to prostitution.

New York City's population approaches 200,000, but fewer than 8 percent of Americans live in cities.

1831   The New York Magdalen Society, founded a year earlier, issues a report estimating 10,000 women in the city—mostly in working-class neighborhoods—were "harlots by choice." Critics lambaste the statistic, and public outcry leads to the society's demise later in the year.

New York State abolishes imprisonment for debt.

Robert Dale Owen and Thomas Skidmore, two central figures in workers' politics, battle over birth control. Owen contends that the working class must limit family size to improve its economic status. Skidmore focuses on the unequal system of property distribution.

1832   Cholera kills thousands in seaport cities and exposes the poor sanitary conditions in working-class neighborhoods.

Charles G. Finney, the leading evangelical preacher of the previous decade, arrives in New York City to become pastor of the Second Free Presbyterian Church. Finney brings western-style revivalism to the big city.

1834   Female factory operatives in Lowell, Massachusetts, strike unsuccessfully for higher wages. They attempt another strike in 1836.

The New York Female Moral Reform Society begins to distribute tracts to prostitutes in working-class neighborhoods and sends visitors to pray with poor women in their homes. Their newspaper, *The Advocate of Moral Reform,* guides middle-class readers through "the pit of corruption."

In Great Britain, Parliament passes the Poor Law Amendment Act, ending local (parish) control of public relief. A national board divides England

and Wales into districts, oversees the erection of workhouses, and requires anyone seeking relief to live within the facility.

1835 In the New York Senate, Colonel Samuel Young, a Democrat from Saratoga County, offers a resolution to end all public relief. It is immediately tabled.

The imposing Blockley almshouse opens outside of Philadelphia, allowing the city to subject all relief applicants to institutional control.

Excoriating abolitionists, Governor George McDuffie of South Carolina argues that southern slaves live far better than impoverished factory operatives. Abolitionists respond that northern workers must help overthrow slavery in order to improve conditions for labor everywhere.

1836 White women in New York start the Association for the Benefit of Colored Orphans and open an asylum for black children the following year.

1837 Economic panic once again creates massive unemployment nationwide and incites mass protests in New York against inflated rents and food prices. The economy remains hobbled through 1842.

1840 Over the previous decade, 600,000 immigrants arrived in the United States. Nearly three times as many will come during the 1840s. The face of the urban poor will become increasingly foreign, which adds nativist sentiment to continued welfare reform efforts.

The Pennsylvania legislature reinstates six-month cash pensions for some of Philadelphia's poor.

Boston Quarterly Review editor Orestes Brownson explains poverty as a function of an irrepressible class conflict between labor and capital. Soon identified with Karl Marx, this argument will gain currency in coming decades.

Questions for Consideration

1. Look closely at the vocabulary used to label the poor. What are the connotations of words like *pauper, intemperate, improvident, idle, dependent,* and *deserving?* What other terms might be added to this list?

2. Why did early republic commentators and policymakers find poverty so alarming? What deeper fears did poverty tap?

3. What motivated those involved in welfare reform? Were reformers optimists who believed in the ability of humans to solve social problems or pessimists who saw crime and danger at every turn?

4. How did ideas of gender and sexuality figure into the discussion of welfare? Were men and women held to different standards as relief recipients? Did the issue of race play an important role in the public debate?

5. Where in the welfare reform debate can we find the voices of the poor? What barriers to upward mobility stood in the way of impoverished people? What relationship did poor men, women, and children have with private and public relief?

6. Where did early republic writers draw the line between the causes and the effects of poverty?

7. Was poverty in the early republic a function of individual moral failings or a flaw in the structure of the economy? Explain.

8. Which solutions offered the most chance of ending the suffering of the poor? Which solutions offered the most promise of ending the burden that poverty placed on taxpayers? Were any of these solutions politically viable?

9. What role did early republic Americans believe that government should play in addressing poverty?

10. Are there lessons from the early republic welfare reform debate that might prove useful to present-day policymakers? Are there dangers in making analogies between the past and the present—for instance, in comparing alcohol abuse in the 1820s to drug abuse in today's inner cities?

Selected Bibliography

OVERVIEWS OF POVERTY AND POOR RELIEF IN THE UNITED STATES

Kenneth L. Kusmer, *Down and Out, On the Road: The Homeless in American History* (New York: Oxford University Press, 2002); Michael Katz, *In the Shadow of the Poorhouse: A Social History of Welfare in America* (New York: Basic Books, 1986); Walter I. Trattner, *From Poor Law to Welfare State: A History of Social Welfare in America*, 5th ed. (New York: Free Press, 1994); Frances Fox Piven and Richard A. Cloward, *Regulating the Poor: The Functions of Public Welfare*, rev. ed. (New York: Vintage Books, 1993).

SPECIFIC LOCAL STUDIES FOR THE EARLY REPUBLIC PERIOD

Priscilla F. Clement, *Welfare and the Poor in the Nineteenth-Century City: Philadelphia, 1800–1854* (Rutherford, N.J.: Fairleigh Dickinson University Press, 1985); John K. Alexander, *Render Them Submissive: Responses to Poverty in Philadelphia, 1760–1800* (Amherst: University of Massachusetts Press, 1980); Robert E. Cray Jr., *Paupers and Poor Relief: New York City and Its Rural Environs, 1700–1830* (Philadelphia: Temple University Press, 1988); Raymond Mohl, *Poverty in New York, 1783–1825* (New York: Oxford University Press, 1971); Barbara L. Bellows, *Benevolence among Slaveholders: Assisting the Poor in Charleston, 1670–1860* (Baton Rouge: Louisiana State University Press, 1993).

LIFE AND LABOR IN WORKING-CLASS NEIGHBORHOODS

Billy G. Smith, *The "Lower Sort": Philadelphia's Laboring People, 1750–1800* (Ithaca: Cornell University Press, 1990); Christine Stansell, *City of Women: Sex and Class in New York, 1789–1860* (New York: Alfred A. Knopf, 1986); Tyler Anbinder, *Five Points: The Nineteenth-Century New York City Neighborhood That Invented Tap Dance, Stole Elections, and Became the World's Most Notorious Slum* (New York: Free Press, 2001); Seth Rockman, "Women's Labor, Gender Ideology, and Working-Class Households in Early Republic Baltimore," *Explorations in Early American Culture* 3 (1999): 174–200; Billy G. Smith, ed., *Life in Early Philadelphia: Documents from the*

172

Revolutionary and Early National Periods (University Park: Pennsylvania State University Press, 1995); Paul Gilje and Howard Rock, *Keepers of the Revolution: New Yorkers at Work in the Early Republic* (Ithaca: Cornell University Press, 1992).

POVERTY AND PUBLIC WELFARE IN THE COLONIAL ERA

Gary B. Nash, "Poverty and Poor Relief in Pre-Revolutionary Philadelphia," *William and Mary Quarterly* 33 (1976): 3–30; Douglas L. Jones, "The Strolling Poor: Transiency in Eighteenth-Century Massachusetts," *Journal of Social History* 8 (1975): 28–54; Allan Kulikoff, "The Progress of Inequality in Revolutionary Boston," *William and Mary Quarterly* 28 (1971): 375–411. More recently, see Ruth Wallis Herndon, *Unwelcome Americans: Living on the Margin in Early New England* (Philadelphia: University of Pennsylvania Press, 2001); Karin Wulf, *Not All Wives: Women of Colonial Philadelphia* (Ithaca: Cornell University Press, 2000), chapter 5; Elaine Forman Crane, *Ebb Tide in New England: Women, Seaports, and Social Change, 1630–1800* (Boston: Northeastern University Press, 1998). On the larger issues of poverty and class in the colonial period, see the essays in Carla G. Pestana and Sharon V. Salinger, eds., *Inequality in Early America* (Hanover, N.H.: University Press of New England, 1999). Drew McCoy addresses anxieties about poverty in republican political thought in *The Elusive Republic: Political Economy in Jeffersonian America* (Chapel Hill: University of North Carolina Press, 1980).

COMPARATIVE STUDIES

Robert Jutte, *Poverty and Deviance in Early Modern Europe* (New York: Cambridge University Press, 1994); Gertrude Himmelfarb, *The Idea of Poverty: England in the Early Industrial Age* (New York: Alfred A. Knopf, 1984); Stuart Woolf, *The Poor in Western Europe in the Eighteenth and Nineteenth Centuries* (London: Methuen, 1986); Peter Mandler, ed., *The Uses of Charity: The Poor on Relief in the Nineteenth-Century Metropolis* (Philadelphia: University of Pennsylvania Press, 1990); Louis Chevalier, *Laboring Classes and Dangerous Classes in Paris during the First Half of the Nineteenth Century*, trans. Frank Jellinek (New York: Howard Fertig, 1973); Tim Hitchcock et al., eds., *Chronicling Poverty: The Voices and Strategies of the English Poor, 1640–1840* (New York: St. Martin's Press, 1997); Heather Shore, *Artful Dodgers: Youth and Crime in Early Nineteenth-Century London* (Woodbridge, UK: Royal Historical Society/Boydell Press, 1999). For a Latin American perspective, see Silvia Marina Arrom, *Containing the Poor: The Mexico City Poor House, 1774–1871* (Durham: Duke University Press, 2000). Camilla Townsend juxtaposes poverty in Baltimore and Guayaquil, Ecuador, in *Tales of Two Cities: Race and Economic Culture in Early Republican North and South America* (Austin: University of Texas Press, 2000).

THE DEVELOPMENT OF CAPITALISM IN THE EARLY REPUBLIC

Paul A. Gilje, ed., *Wages of Independence: Capitalism in the Early American Republic* (Madison, Wisc.: Madison House, 1997); American Social History Project, *Who Built America? Working People and the Nation's Economy, Politics, Culture, and Society*, vol. 1 (New York: Worth, 2000); Paul E. Johnson, "The Market Revolution," in Mary K. Cayton et al., eds., *Encyclopedia of American Social History* (New York: Charles Scribner's Sons, 1993), vol. 1, 545–60. For a broader social context, see Charles Sellers, *The Market Revolution: Jacksonian America, 1815–1846* (New York: Oxford University Press, 1991); Gordon Wood, *The Radicalism of the American Revolution* (New York: Alfred A. Knopf, 1992); Louis Masur, *1831, Year of Eclipse* (New York: Hill and Wang, 2001).

RELIGIOUS AND SECULAR REFORM

Steven Mintz, *Moralists & Modernizers: America's Pre–Civil War Reformers* (Baltimore: Johns Hopkins University Press, 1995); Ronald G. Walters, *American Reformers, 1815–1860*, rev. ed. (New York: Hill and Wang, 1997); Curtis Johnson, *Redeeming America: Evangelicals and the Road to Civil War* (Chicago: Ivan R. Dee, 1993); Lori Ginzberg, *Women in Antebellum Reform* (Wheeling, Ill.: Harlan Davidson, 2000). For more detailed studies, see Robert Abzug, *Cosmos Crumbling: American Reform and the Religious Imagination* (New York: Oxford University Press, 1994); Lori Ginzberg, *Women and the Work of Benevolence: Morality, Politics, and Class in the Nineteenth-Century United States* (New Haven: Yale University Press, 1990); Bruce Dorsey, *Reforming Men and Women: Gender in the Antebellum City* (Ithaca: Cornell University Press, 2002); Conrad E. Wright, *The Transformation of Charity in Post-Revolutionary New England* (Boston: Northeastern University Press, 1992); Carroll Smith-Rosenberg, *Religion and the Rise of the American City: The New York City Mission Movement, 1812–1870* (Ithaca: Cornell University Press, 1971); Paul Boyer, *Urban Masses and Moral Order in America, 1820–1920* (Cambridge: Harvard University Press, 1978); William H. Pease and Jane H. Pease, *The Web of Progress: Private Values and Public Styles in Boston and Charleston, 1828–1843* (New York: Oxford University Press, 1985); Anne Firor Scott, *Natural Allies: Women's Associations in American History* (Urbana: University of Illinois Press, 1992); Suzanne Lebsock, *The Free Women of Petersburg: Status and Culture in a Southern Town, 1784–1860* (New York: W.W. Norton, 1984).

EARLY REPUBLIC REHABILITATIVE INSTITUTIONS

David J. Rothman, *The Discovery of the Asylum: Social Order and Disorder in the New Republic* (Boston: Little, Brown, 1971); Michael Meranze, *Laboratories of Virtue: Punishment, Revolution, and Authority in Philadelphia,*

1760–1835 (Chapel Hill: University of North Carolina Press, 1996). For a broader perspective, see Michel Foucault, *Discipline and Punish: The Birth of the Prison,* trans. Alan Sheridan (New York: Pantheon Books, 1977). Two important studies of the American educational system are David Nasaw, *Schooled to Order: A Social History of Public Schooling in the United States* (New York: Oxford University Press, 1979); Carl F. Kaestle, *Pillars of the Republic: Common Schools and American Society, 1780–1860* (New York: Hill and Wang, 1983).

WORKING-CLASS REFORM AND POLITICS

Edward Pessen, *Most Uncommon Jacksonians, The Radical Leaders of the Early Labor Movement* (Albany: State University of New York Press, 1967); Jamie L. Bronstein, *Land Reform and Working-Class Experience in Britain and the United States, 1800–1862* (Stanford: Stanford University Press, 1999); Sean Wilentz, *Chants Democratic: New York City and the Rise of the American Working Class, 1788–1850* (New York: Oxford University Press, 1984); William Sutton, *Journeymen for Jesus: Evangelical Artisans Confront Capitalism in Jacksonian Baltimore* (University Park: Pennsylvania State University Press, 1998); Martin J. Burke, *The Conundrum of Class: Public Discourse on the Social Order in America* (Urbana: University of Chicago Press, 1995), chapter 4. For 1790s ideas of economic justice, see Seth Cotlar, "Radical Concepts of Property Rights and Economic Justice in the Early Republic: The Trans-Atlantic Dimension," *Explorations in Early American Culture* 4 (2000): 191–219.

EARLY REPUBLIC WELFARE DOCUMENTS

In 1971, David Rothman collected early republic welfare documents for the Arno Press series *Poverty U.S.A.* Titles include *The Charitable Impulse in Eighteenth-Century America*; *The Jacksonians on the Poor; The Almshouse Experience;* and *Joseph Tuckerman on the Elevation of the Poor.* These texts have now been republished by Ayer Company Publishers. The annual reports of countless benevolent organizations, along with many charity sermons, are reproduced through 1820 in the *Early American Imprints* microprint series available at many college and university libraries. Similarly, the working-class newspapers of the 1820s and 1830s have been microfilmed in the *American Periodical Series.* Many official state reports on public welfare, as well as reports of the Pennsylvania Society for the Promotion of Public Economy and the New York Society for the Prevention of Pauperism, have been microfilmed in the *Goldsmiths'-Kress Library of Economic Literature.* For a European perspective, see the new edition of Alexis de Tocqueville's 1830s *Memoir on Pauperism: With an Introduction by Gertrude Himmelfarb* (Chicago: Ivan R. Dee, 1997), an early lament on welfare dependence. The massive British literature on poverty in cities like London and Manchester has been collected in John Marriott and Masaie Matsumura, eds., *The Metropolitan Poor: Semi-Factual Accounts, 1795–1910*, 6 vols. (London: Pickering and Chatto, 1999). Count Rumford's plans for institutionalizing the Bavarian poor are in Sanborn Brown, ed. *Collected Works of Count Rumford* (Cambridge: Belknap Press of Harvard University Press, 1970), vol. 5.

Index

education. *See also* public education
  alleviating poverty through, 46, 63
  in almshouses, 105, 121
  common schools, 142–43
  comprehensive system, 139
  in craft skills, 166
  of orphans, 144–45
  recommendations for, 142–45
  school attendance, 42
  taxes and, 144
eleemosynary, defined, 53*n*
Ely, Ezra Stiles, 28, 167
  "Preacher to the Poor in New York,"
    75–83
Embargo Act, 166
employment
  in almshouses, 106*f*
  of children, 45, 81, 85, 100, 160
  erroneous opinions about, 147
  in factories, 157–60, 169
  industrialization and, 9, 16, 25
  lack of, 16, 38, 43–44, 99, 148,
    149, 161
  providing opportunities for, 47, 55
  taxes and, 144
  on whaling voyages, 89
  willingness to work, 43–44, 99
England. *See* Great Britain

factory employment
  of children, 160
  as wage slavery, 160
  of women, 157–60, 169
Female Association for the Relief of
  Sick Poor, and for the Education
  of Such Female Children as Do
  Not Belong to, or Are Not
  Provided for, by Any Religious
  Society, 166
female-headed households, 10–11
Female Hebrew Benevolent Society,
  167
Female Humane Association (FHA),
  165
  charity school, 73–74
Female Society, Second Presbyterian
  Church, Philadelphia, 17
Female Society for Relief and
  Employment of the Poor, 13, 165
Finney, Charles G., 169
fires, urban, 80

Fitzhugh, George, 29
Five Points, New York, 50*f*
Foss, Catherine (Baltimore
  Almshouse), 116
Foss, John (Baltimore Almshouse),
  116
Foss, William Henry (Baltimore
  Almshouse), 117
foster parenting, 7
Free Enquirer, 26, 28, 139
free will, 12
Friendly Society of St. Thomas's
  African Church, 67–69, 165

gender roles, 14
Gervin, Hugh (Baltimore Almshouse),
  113
Gilbreath, William (Baltimore
  Almshouse), 116
Gillet, Timothy, 12
girls' schools, 13, 17, 73–74, 166
Gore, Mary (Baltimore Almshouse),
  117
Gray, Matilda (Baltimore Almshouse),
  118
Great Britain
  immigrants from, 23–24
  industrial development, 9
  Poor Laws, 22, 23, 169–70
  poverty relief programs, 5
Griffith, Thomas, 20
Griscom, John, 49
Guardians of the Poor, Philadelphia
  Report of the Board, 126–30

Hamilton, Alexander, 131, 165
Hammond, James Henry, 29
Harman, Philip (Baltimore
  Almshouse), 113–14
Hart, Nathaniel C., 18
Hartford, Connecticut, 2
head taxes, for immigrants, 23–24, 129
hod carriers, 148–51
Holmes, Abiel, 15
House of Refuge, New York. *See* New
  York House of Refuge
House of Refuge, Philadelphia, 93*f*
houses of industry, 6
  Boston, 107–11, 168
  civil liberties and, 23
  Philadelphia, 165